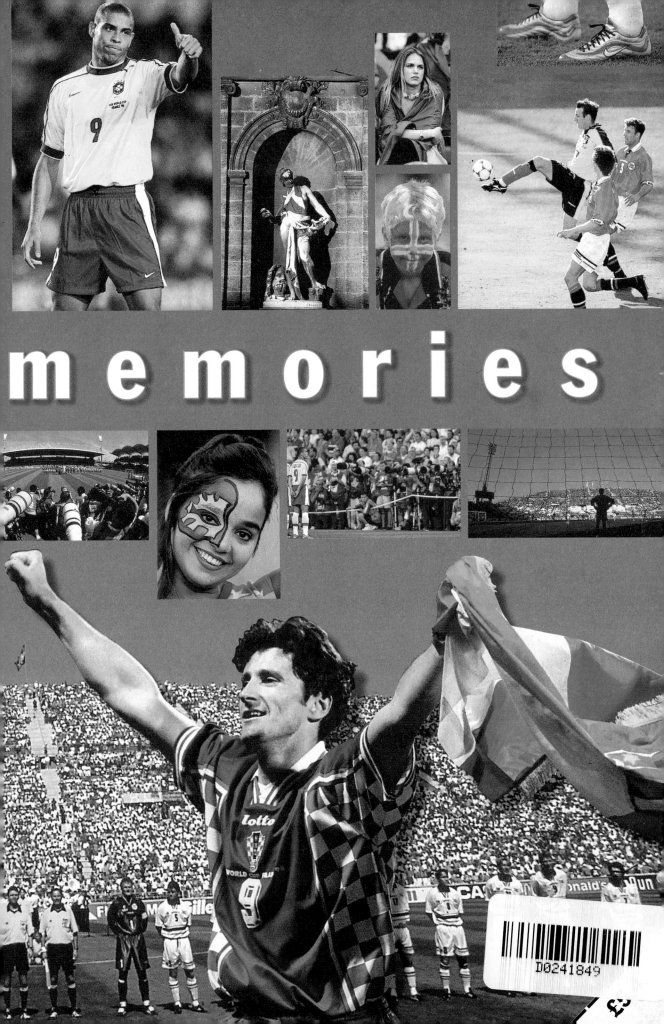

memories

topical times football book 1999

CO

ntents

fast forward!

It didn't take Liverpool's MICHAEL OWEN long to make his mark!

SUCH has been Michael Owen's amazing progress that it is already hard to think of a Liverpool team without him. Less than two years after making his debut as a 17-year-old, he is an England international and very much part of the furniture at Anfield.

His name already sits quite happily alongside the elite list of great Liverpool strikers which includes Roger Hunt, Kevin Keegan, Kenny Dalglish, Ian Rush and Robbie Fowler.

A prodigious goalscorer in youth and reserve sides, Owen was viewed as a good long-term prospect. A slow introduction to the rigours of first-team football looked likely.

With former German internationalist Karl-Heinz Riedle alongside Robbie Fowler, there was no reason to over-use Owen's raw talents. Owen, though, had other ideas.

Injury and a loss of form saw Fowler experience the poorest campaign in his career, while Riedle struggled to make his expected impact. Owen stepped into the breach, relegated Riedle to the bench and went on to overshadow the troubled Fowler.

It did not take long for England coach, Glenn Hoddle, to sit up and take notice. In February, aged 18 years and 59 days, he broke Duncan Edwards' 42-year-old record to become the youngest player to play for his country this century when he lined up to face Chile.

Heady stuff for a teenager, but the Chester-born youngster has a maturity beyond his years and has not been fazed by his sudden rise to fame.

"I have tried to keep as level-headed as possible," says Michael.

"I'm just a normal person who happens to play football for a living.

"I know the spotlight will always be on me as long as I play for Liverpool. But this club looks after me very well. "Make no mistake, if I was to get too big for my boots there would be a few people on my back straight away." Despite having taken everything in his stride, Owen admits that even he was surprised at the speed of his elevation to first-team status.

"I didn't expect my appearances to hit double figures last season, never mind my goals tally," he adds. "The boss, Roy Evans, told me that he did not intend to play me throughout the

> ## "I didn't expect my appearances to hit double figures last season, never mind my goals tally."

season. He said he would leave me out sometimes, not because of the way I was playing, but due to my age and the fact that he thought I might not be able to last a full Premiership season.

"A lot of clubs nowadays are bringing their young players through carefully to ensure that they are not asking too much too soon. It's nice to know that the club is looking after you that way.

"I was rested for a while early on but whenever the team was picked, I wanted to be named in it and I wanted to play in every game. When I did get back into the first team, I kept my place.

"One of

the most pleasing things was that I was in on merit. Even when we were free from injuries and suspensions, I wasn't left out.

"It helped that my goals kept coming so I didn't suffer from a barren run. I scored a few hat-tricks but most of my other goals came in tight matches."

Owen knows that reaching the top was the easy part. Staying there will be a great deal more difficult.

"I am aware that some people are just waiting for me to have a fall," adds Michael. "That doesn't worry me. Having setbacks is all part of learning the game.

I improved as the season went on. I am a much wiser player than the one who played in the opening game of last season against Wimbledon.

"I don't think I can put my finger on one particular area of my game that has improved. But in terms of the general picture, I was pleased that I dealt with many of the problems that were posed on the pitch.

"The first thing you learn when you are in the first team is that you have to make your own decisions. The game is too quick and too demanding for team-mates to help you out all the time.

"When I was playing in the youth team or the reserves, the manager could get his message across by shouting from the sidelines. But he cannot really be heard when there are 40,000 people there."

While it is his precocious ability to find the net that has grabbed the attention, Owen does not see that as the main weapon in his armoury. He believes he is a creative footballer as well.

He ends, "People only saw the goals I scored. But there was more to my game than that. I've always

been a player who likes to get in crosses for others.

"One of my best games for Liverpool was against Aston Villa. I didn't score, but made two goals and was brought down for a penalty.

"I'm not one to keep goal records. I know roughly what I've scored, but I don't know my record off pat." ■

Michael's debut for England v Chile.

dennis bergkamp
arsenal

headlines!

a

RSENAL'S Ray Parlour has something that's quite unusual amongst his team-mates... a London accent.

The Gunners have invested heavily in foreign talent over the last couple of years, including Dutch superstars Dennis Bergkamp and Marc Overmars, Austrian keeper Alex Manninger but most particularly Frenchmen.

It was inevitable that when Arsene Wenger took charge at Highbury, some of his fellow countrymen would follow him into the famous marble halls. Patrick Vieira, Emmanuel Petit and Nicolas Anelka led the way across the English Channel.

At first, the babble of different languages seemed to create nothing but confusion in the Arsenal dressing-room. It took a while for all the players to get on the same wavelength and speak the same language.

Ray Parlour soon realised that playing football was the best way to communicate with his overseas team-mates. That's one language they all

french

How the gloss was put on RAY PARLOUR'S season!

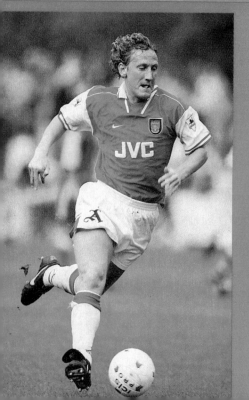

had in common.

"Good communication is vital out on a football pitch," says Parlour. "You have to know what the other players are doing.

"So it was no coincidence that we started to get better and better last season as the French lads improved their English. It really did make a difference in games.

"They all went off and worked hard with their language teachers after training. Then of course they picked up a bit of Cockney rhyming slang from me too!

"I really enjoyed playing alongside Patrick Vieira and Manu Petit in our midfield. They just got better and better as the season went on."

Last season also marked a watershed for Parlour himself. He shook off his bad-boy image off the pitch and started to become much more consistent on it.

For several seasons, he was in and out of the Arsenal team. Then, at last, he found a manager who really believed in his ability.

"Arsene Wenger showed real faith in me and gave me a good long run in the team. It was then I really started to believe in myself and definitely played my best football.

"Before that I was in and out of the team all the time and couldn't get myself established. Consistency was what I really needed and when that started to come, things moved very fast in my career."

Parlour was beginning to make a big impression, not least on Glenn

Emmanuel Petit

10

polish!

Hoddle. The England boss first brought him into the B squad then he made it into the full squad.

"That was a wonderful honour for me and quite a shock too," says Ray.

"I was surprised enough to be included in the B team. To be called up for the full squad was something else again.

"Unfortunately, the rigours of the season caught up with me on both occasions. When I reported for the B team game, it looked like I'd been in a

> ## "Then I really started to believe in myself and definitely played my best football."

war because my body was black and blue from a bruising Premiership encounter with Chelsea.

"Thankfully, I still managed to play the game and I must have done well because Glenn Hoddle then brought

me into his full squad for a friendly in Switzerland. It was very frustrating when I had to drop out because of a niggling hamstring injury.

"Pulling on an England shirt at any level is a great thrill. I would never turn down the chance to play for my country if I was fit.

"Nobody wants to drop out of an England squad. I just hope I can do my bit to help England to the European Championships in the year 2000.

"Injuries are inevitable in the tough domestic programme we have in England. I've never been one to hold back on the way I play so I'm bound to pick up a few bumps and bruises."

Last year couldn't have gone much better for Ray. He played a major part in Arsenal's campaign for the Double, took a major step up the international ladder and put his hard-drinking days right behind him.

Parlour got himself into a few unfortunate scrapes as a youngster. But now he's a family man with two children, looking ahead to a bright future.

"I knew I had to get my act

Arsene-al Wenger

together," says Ray. "If I hadn't, I would certainly have regretted it later.

"It's been great to be part of a successful Arsenal team over the last year. Let's just hope it continues.

"The foreign lads were all delighted when we reached the FA Cup Final last season. I was lucky enough to have played in the 1993 Final but for most of the newcomers it was their first big Wembley occasion.

"That's what we want more of at Arsenal now. Once you get in the winning habit, you never want to break it." ■

CARLING CHAMPIONS

all change!

THE TURNING POINT OF ARSENAL'S SEASON WAS NEITHER THEIR HOME NOR THEIR AWAY VICTORY OVER MANCHESTER UNITED; NOR WAS IT ONE OF THEIR CONFIDENCE-BOOSTING 5-0 THRASHINGS OF BARNSLEY AND WIMBLEDON, NOR THE SPARKLING 4-1 VICTORY AT BLACKBURN. THE KEY TO ARSENAL'S PREMIERSHIP TRIUMPH WAS ACTUALLY A HOME DEFEAT BY BLACKBURN ROVERS.

tHE 3-1 reverse, in December 1997, which was the lowest point of an eight-match run containing only two wins, produced a bout of individual and collective soul-searching at Highbury.

The result was a four-month period without a defeat, climaxing with a run of ten consecutive victories that effectively wrenched the trophy from the hands of Manchester United.

After losing to Blackburn, the team held a no-holds-barred meeting at which problems were aired and put right.

It was also a personal turning point for skipper Tony Adams.

"That defeat served as a big motivating force for me," recalls Adams. "I knew how upset the fans were. I looked at the Arsenal web-site on the Internet afterwards, and read the comments — some about me. It didn't make good reading.

"I react to criticism because I always want to prove critics wrong. I knew I had to do something.

"I'd been carrying injuries for two years, and knew there were question marks against me. My pride wouldn't let me be an also-ran."

The Arsenal captain has since admitted that he was close to calling it a day at that point. But he and manager Arsene Wenger decided the England centre-half would benefit from a few weeks of rest and rehabilitation in France.

Adams returned to Highbury refreshed in mind and body, to regain his finest form for Arsenal and England. In his absence, the team was starting to put together the long unbeaten run.

His return to the side was the final piece in the jigsaw. Arsenal never looked back from that Blackburn defeat until the title was won.

But there were other significant moments. One was the home match against Crystal Palace, on the 21st of February. On the Saturday morning, manager Wenger could barely find eleven fit players to field a team. Seven first-team regulars were ruled out through injury or suspension.

In the end, one unknown made his first-team debut, reserves filled

●Tim Sherwood scores for Blackburn

● Gilles Grimandi

12

The same could be said for every player at Arsenal.

The win over Everton set the scene for the Double. Arsenal's Cup Final opponents were Kenny Dalglish's Newcastle United, and it was two of Highbury's foreign legion who grabbed the glory. Goals from Marc Overmars (below) and Nicolas Anelka ensured a two-nil win for the North London side and gave the Gunners the Double for the first time since 1972. ■

six other places, and three untested youngsters were on the bench for the first time. Arsenal scraped home 1-0 thanks to a goal by reserve defender Gilles Grimandi.

"That was potentially very tricky, but the youngsters who came in did ever so well," says first-team coach Pat Rice.

"Gilles Grimandi's goal was very significant in our Championship victory."

Obviously, the two wins over Manchester United were highly important. The first, at home in November 1997, was secured by a late winning goal from David Platt (above), after United had pulled back from 0-2, to equalise.

Arsenal had gone into the match without three key players, all suspended — Dennis Bergkamp, Manu Petit, and Steve Bould.

"I am disappointed about the suspensions," said manager Arsene Wenger. "We are a competitive team, which is part of the Arsenal spirit. But we are not a violent team."

in Arsenal's path was the visit to Blackburn Rovers, who were themselves chasing a UEFA Cup place. But Dennis Bergkamp, returning from a two-match suspension, scored within 75 seconds, and Ray Parlour added two more inside the first 15 minutes. The Gunners cruised to a 4-1 win that virtually removed all doubts about the Premiership issue, even if the players were taking nothing for granted.

The title was eventually wrapped up in a comprehensive victory over Everton at Highbury. Fittingly, skipper Adams sealed the win with a spectacular goal.

"I proved to myself during my rehab period in France that I was fit again," he says. "I went out to prove to everyone that my standards were as high as they'd ever been."

The second, at Old Trafford in mid-March, finally tipped the balance in Arsenal's favour. A Marc Overmars goal (above) defeated the reigning Champions.

"We never thought about the Championship until after the win at Old Trafford, which put it into our own hands," says Rice.

The final difficult hurdle standing

> " When I won the Championship in Holland, with Ajax, there were some games we knew we would win no matter how we played," says Marc Overmars.
>
> "It is not like than in England. Every Premiership team, even the one at the bottom of the table, is capable of winning matches.
>
> "You cannot afford to be over-confident. You have to treat every game the same. "

who wants to be a
millionaire?

mANCHESTER UNITED defender Jaap Stam has a million reasons to win the Premiership and Champions League with the Old Trafford club. The Dutchman, who arrived at United in a £10.75 million transfer from PSV Eindhoven on the eve of last summer's World Cup, gave up a personal fortune to allow him to pursue his bid for glory with Alex Ferguson's team.

United, like many other Premiership clubs, have seen moves for top foreign players scuppered by excessive wage demands. In Stam's case, however, the player gave up a huge windfall just to sign for United.

Old Trafford chairman Martin Edwards described Stam's attitude as 'very rare in the modern game.'

Stam, who played a major part in Holland's progression into the semi-finals of France 98, admits that he had to forfeit his million pound bonus in order to fulfil his dream of playing for Manchester United.

Jaap reveals, "It's true that I sacrificed a lot of money to come to United. I had an agreement with PSV that I could take a percentage of any transfer fee that they received for me.

"As United's bid was so high, I would have made an awful lot of money if I had stuck to my guns.

"We would have been talking about more than a million pounds, but I was willing to forego that to ensure that the move came off. The two clubs were too far apart on a valuation until I offered to waive my right to the money.

"I never had second thoughts about doing it. I have agreed a seven-year contract with United, so if things go as well as I hope and expect, I will be rewarded anyway.

"Money wasn't my objective when I decided to leave PSV for Old Trafford. I wanted to sign for Manchester United because I enjoy the football they play and I wanted to play in England.

"My only ambition as a United player is to win a lot of trophies. They didn't win the Championship last season but I'm not worried about that happening again.

"I'm pretty confident that trophies will continue to come to this club, starting with this season."

Stam has been described by many in the game as the best defender in Europe. To get their man, United had to pay a world record fee for a defender. Jaap is aware of the pressure that tag will bring, but he admits that United had no option but to pay the huge fee.

He goes on, "I could do nothing about my transfer fee. PSV were right to get the highest possible price for me and United had to pay it. I was under contract to Eindhoven and they didn't have to sell me.

"It is a lot of money and the pressure is on me to justify the fee, but I wouldn't expect anything else.

"I have played at the top level for a few years now and that in itself brings pressure and expectation. I think it is normal, though, for people to expect great things from you if you have cost their club a lot of money.

"It's quite something to be the costliest defender in the world, but I'm not too bothered by it because it is simply a result of market forces in modern football.

"I'm just glad that United were willing to pay the fee for me. As a kid, I adored United and it's a great feeling to be playing for them. It's a dream to be part of the club.

"I think the whole of England expected United to go further than the last eight in the Champions League last season. After what they did to Feyenoord in the group stages, a lot of people back in Holland believed United could win it. Unfortunately, it wasn't to be.

"I'm aware that United are desperate to win the Champions League. It is over 30 years since they last won the European Cup, but the team we have now is good enough to end that wait."

better late

FOOTBALL is said to be a game of opinions and if any man can vouch for that statement it is Newcastle United's Warren Barton.

The former Wimbledon man became the costliest defender in Britain when he quit The Crazy Gang for Kevin Keegan's Newcastle in the summer of 1995.

On arriving at St James' Park, Barton settled in without fuss and his early months at the club suggested that Keegan had spent well.

Barton became a key figure as Newcastle took the Premiership by storm. The rebuilt team, which also included fellow new boys David Ginola and Les Ferdinand, set a breathtaking pace at the top of the Premiership and seemed certain to deliver the first Championship on Tyneside since 1927.

However, as the record books now show, Newcastle began to falter and they were overtaken by eventual Champions Manchester United in a nerve-shredding title run-in.

Unfortunately for Barton, he was to become the fall guy for Newcastle's failure.

His Newcastle career caved in on a fateful March afternoon at Highbury. A 2-0 defeat at the hands of Arsenal saw the Magpies slip to second in the table. Barton was criticised for his performance and he did not start another game under Keegan.

He had been an ever-present until the Arsenal game, but his next start did not come until Kenny Dalglish succeeded Keegan as manager ten months later.

Under Dalglish, Warren has resurrected his Newcastle career. He admits that times were hard as Tyneside's

forgotten man, but he came through it because he realised just how lucky he was.

Warren reveals, "I had a difficult time for a while after falling out of favour with the former manager, Kevin Keegan.

"Everybody sees that Arsenal game as the one that cost me my place, but I don't know if it was just one game. Everybody makes mistakes. You just have to learn to live with them.

"Whatever the reasons were, it was the start of a long period in which I didn't get a picture. I did that during my time out of the team and I realised how lucky I was to be at such a big club.

"Also, being a part of The Crazy Gang at Wimbledon helped me through the problems. It might be a jokey nickname, but being part of it gives you a valuable sense of perspective.

"It may sound strange, but I felt very fortunate. I wasn't playing, but I wasn't injured so I could still train. I'm sure Alan Shearer would have swapped his six-month injury lay-off last season for mine.

"The easiest thing for me to do would have been to walk away from Newcastle, but that was the last thing I wanted. I had fought long and hard to play for a big club, so I wasn't going to throw in the towel at the first setback.

"Former Wimbledon team-mates Robbie Earle and Scott Fitzgerald were always there for me on the other end of the phone.

"It wasn't an easy time, but there are positive aspects to come out of it. I certainly believe I am a better player and a better person now."

Barton's patient, professional approach may be rare in the modern game, but it did not convince Keegan to recall him to the first team. Not until Dalglish stepped in did Warren's fortunes take an upturn.

The man who had guided both Liverpool and Blackburn Rovers to the Championship turned out to be a long-time admirer of Barton. Warren couldn't have wished for a better man to succeed Keegan.

Warren goes on, "As soon as Kenny Dalglish arrived at the club, he put me back in the team and my Newcastle career was back on the rails again. From not playing at all, I was suddenly a regular again.

"I can't explain why he suddenly drafted me in, but I do know that he had kept tabs on me for a number of years. I'm really playing for him at the third time of asking.

"I was told by Wimbledon that he had tried to buy me for Liverpool shortly before he left Anfield in 1991. There was also speculation linking me with Blackburn during his time as manager there.

"I'm just pleased that I have had the opportunity to play for him at Newcastle. He has given me another crack of the whip at this club and as long as I am here, I will do my best to repay him." ∎

than never
Patience paid off for Newcastle's
WARREN BARTON

look-in with the first team. The fact we had no reserve team compounded things for me because I had no opportunity to keep match-fit or get my confidence going.

"It didn't feel good to be out of the side, but you have to accept the highs and lows. I have no quarrel with Kevin Keegan. I still have a lot of respect for him.

"He never said to me that I wasn't good enough and I wasn't frozen out by him. He was always available if I needed to speak to him. Unfortunately, I just didn't figure in his plans.

"There was never any question of me rocking the boat and asking to leave, though. Maybe my upbringing in the game has taught me different values. I have had to overcome knocks throughout my career, right back to the time when I was rejected by Leyton Orient as a youngster.

"You learn to take setbacks. My experience has taught me to take a step back when things aren't going so well and look at the wider

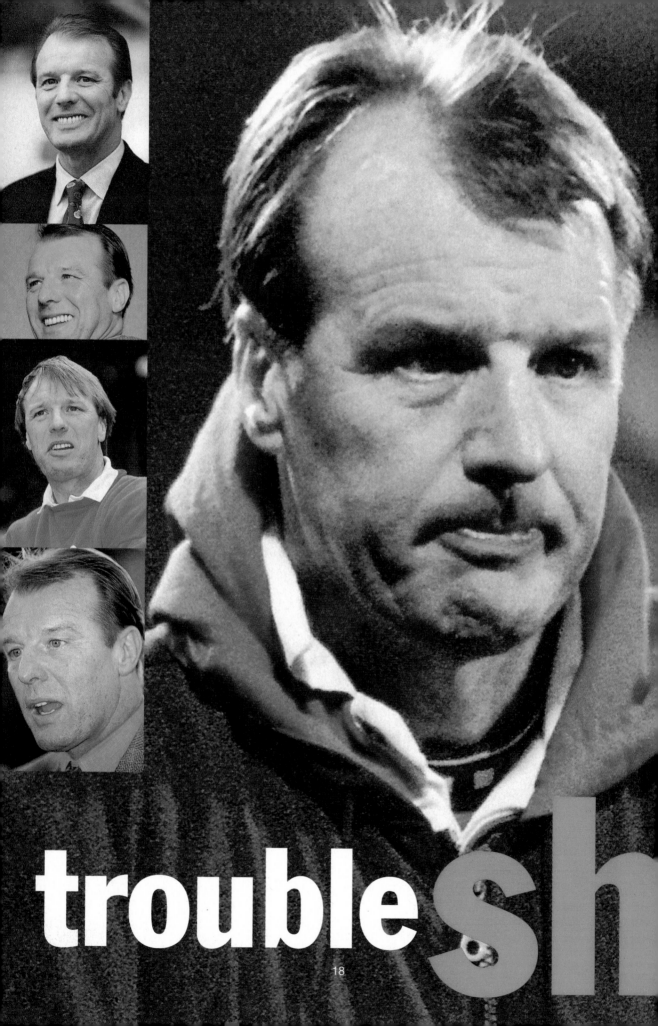

troublesh

When the going gets tough DAVE BASSETT gets going!

NOTTINGHAM FOREST boss Dave Bassett is arguably the most battle-hardened of the current stock of managers.

Bassett has spent most of his 17-year managerial career acting as a trouble-shooter in some of the toughest jobs in football.

Harry, as he is affectionately known in the game, has not managed a so-called big club and has had none of his achievements laid on a plate. He has had to fight for his successes.

During his time, he has taken over at several clubs where morale had hit rock bottom. He had to contend with boardroom upheaval, revolts on the terraces and a poor team on the pitch.

Bassett has been forced into making some difficult decisions in an effort to turn those clubs around. With the exception of a short stay at Watford, he is held in high regard by all his previous clubs and their supporters.

"I am inclined to go into war zones," says Dave. "I don't like wars, I prefer to work in harmony with everyone, but you can stay in the comfort zone too long.

"Sometimes you have to rise to new challenges. That means you will often make unpleasant decisions."

Bassett has never shirked his responsibilities and has been forced into making some hard decisions to turn around ailing clubs.

He joined Forest's backroom staff when morale was low and the club were spiralling towards relegation from the Premiership. He took over the managerial reins the following season and one of his first decisions was to let inspirational skipper Stuart Pearce leave for Newcastle.

He risked the wrath of the Forest faithful, but in an action that was much appreciated by Pearce and many others inside the game, he refused to stand in the way of Pearce's World Cup ambitions.

The Forest support accepted Bassett's decision. They looked at his track record, reputation for honesty and integrity and gave him their full support.

"Supporters like it if you are straightforward with them," adds Dave. "They always knew where I stood and when I left a club, for whatever reason, I never hid the truth.

"I like to think that I am appreciated at my former clubs, not just for bringing them some success, but because I was genuinely liked when I was there."

Indeed, it is a rare thing in football management for a person to be on such good terms with his former clubs.

On a trip to First Division promotion rivals Sheffield United last season, he was presented with a tankard with the heart-felt inscription, 'Thanks for the memories.'

"I had eight great years at Sheffield," says Dave. "I left on good terms, but I left Wimbledon and Palace on good terms, too.

"When I joined Palace, they were 16th in the First Division and when I left they had reached the play-off finals, so there was a vast improvement.

"Wimbledon fans still chant, 'There's only one Harry Bassett.' "

Bassett has had few failures in a career which has perhaps lacked the major honours that his ability deserves.

He has had to sit back and watch big-name players with no managerial experience take short-cuts to take over at many top clubs.

"Some people with designer names come into management and move up the ladder more quickly than managers who do not have a big playing reputation," he goes on.

"I am not jealous. I have had a good career and learned a lot in my time as a manager.

"Of course, I would have preferred to have had more success, perhaps to have reached a few cup finals and managed a side in Europe. But the clubs I have been with have dictated that was not to be.

"I am not looked upon as a manager who will win a European trophy. In fact, no one has given me the chance to win the Premiership. I am perceived as a man who can win a side promotion and I am proud of that.

"Perhaps I should have had the chance to manage a top club. In my first season with Wimbledon in the old First Division, we finished sixth and reached the quarter-finals of the FA Cup. I kept Sheffield United in the top flight for four seasons.

"But neither club were ever serious challengers because we could not take the next step forward. That is because we could not afford to buy the players we needed. Let's face it, money is the dominant factor.

"I had chances to go to Aston Villa and Chelsea, but turned them down. People said I was wrong, but they did not know the pros and cons involved. For instance, Chelsea were not the same Chelsea then as we have now. The club only took off when Glenn Hoddle was in charge.

"Some people said I was silly to leave Premiership-bound Palace to come to Forest, who were odds-on to be relegated. But I had my reasons and I have no regrets." ■

> "Sometimes you have to rise to new challenges. That means you will often make unpleasant decisions."

ooter!

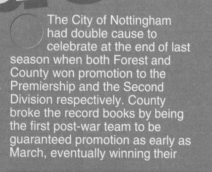

double tops

The City of Nottingham had double cause to celebrate at the end of last season when both Forest and County won promotion to the Premiership and the Second Division respectively. County broke the record books by being the first post-war team to be guaranteed promotion as early as March, eventually winning their league by a massive 17 points. Forest, on the other hand, had a tighter fight and triumphed over their nearest rivals by just 3 points.

While the players of both teams celebrated in style, the managers who guided them to promotion — County's Sam Allardyce and Forest boss Dave Bassett — relaxed with their trophies...and a bottle or two of bubbly!

what do you remember about
the world cup?

FRANCE 98

1. Name the Scotland player who scored an own goal against Brazil in the opening game of the tournament. BOYD

2. In which city did England play their opening match? MARSEILLES

3. Which Dutch player became the world's most expensive defender just before the Finals? STAM

4. Which Brazilian entered the competition as FIFA's World Player Of The Year? RONALDO

5. Name the Chelsea defender who scored a last minute winner for Romania against England. PETRESCU

6. Which England player came off the bench to score in that game? OWEN

7. Which team was nicknamed the 'Reggae Boyz'? JAMAICA

8. Name the Celtic player who was sent off in Scotland's defeat by Morocco. BURLEY

9. How many quarter-final ties went to extra-time and penalties? ONE

10. Which country put England out of the competition in a penalty shoot-out? ARGENTINA

11. Name the two England players who had their spot-kicks saved. 1. INCE 2. BATTY

12. Who scored the only hat-trick of the Finals? BATISTUTA

13. Name the Finals venue especially built for the tournament. STADE DE FRANCE

14. Which former Newcastle player was sent home early from the Colombian squad? ASPRILLA

15. Name the former Tottenham striker who captained Germany during the Finals. KLINSMANN

16. Which two countries ended up with no points from their group matches? USA & JAPAN

17. Which brothers helped Denmark through to the quarter-final stages? MICHAEL & BRIAN LAUDRUP

18. Who became Holland's record goal scorer during the tournament? BERGKAMP

19. Who scored England's goals in their two-nil win over Colombia? ANDERTON & BECKHAM

20. Who won the Golden Boot as the tournament's top scorer

and how many goals did he score? SUCKER (6)

21. Whose last match as a TV commentator was the World Cup Final? BRIAN MOORE

22. Which Premiership club provided most players at the World Cup finals? CHELSEA

23. Which team went out of the competition after winning a game 6-1? SPAIN

1998

See question 19

answers

1.Tom Boyd. **2.**Marseilles. **3.**Jaap Stam. **4.**Ronaldo. **5.**Dan Petrescu. **6.**Michael Owen. **7.**Jamaica. **8.**Craig Burley. **9.**One. Italy v France. **10.**Argentina. **11.**Paul Ince and David Batty. **12.**Gabriel Batistuta. **13.**The Stade de France. **14.**Faustino Asprilla. **15.** Jurgen Klinsmann. **16.**Japan and the USA. **17.**Michael and Brian Laudrup. **18.**Dennis Bergkamp. **19.**Darren Anderton and David Beckham. **20.**Davor Suker (6 goals) **21.**Brian Moore. **22.**Chelsea (11). **23.**Spain.

dream teams

blues

r. carlos
brazil

b. laudrup
denmark

henry
france

blanc
france

del piero
italy

ronaldo
brazil

chilavert
paraguay

adams
england

zidane
france

thuram
france

raul
spain

Most of the world's greatest players were on show in the World Cup in France 98. And every fan picked his or her own Dream Team from that dazzling array of stars. But we at the Topical Times went one better. We selected TWO all-star squads — then arranged a match between them! This is how we think such a game might have turned out...

reds

bergkamp
holland

okocha
nigeria

west
nigeria

cannavaro
italy

owen
england

ortega
argentina

schmeichel
denmark

desailly
france

denilson
brazil

lizarazu
france

overmars
holland

Turn the page for the Dream Teams' match report.

substitutes

a capacity crowd of 105,000 in a sun-drenched Stade de France saw Holland's Dennis Bergkamp kick off in the match which had captured the imagination of the football world.

After a cagey opening ten minutes when both sides sized each other up, the Blues were first to show any initiative when a long ball from England's Tony Adams sought out Thierry Henry wide on the right. However, a crashing tackle from his French compatriot Desailly knocked the ball out for a throw. Roberto Carlos's long throw was easily fielded by the Reds' goalkeeper and captain, Peter Schmeichel.

Then the match suddenly burst into life. A seemingly lost cause was chased down the left by Dutch flyer Marc Overmars. Lilian Thuram ushered him down towards the corner flag, but a neat back-heel from Overmars found Ariel Ortega and he hit it first-time to the Blues' far post. Chilavert got a hand to it but could only knock it down to the feet of Bergkamp. The Dutch hit-man didn't hesitate, and hit a left-foot volley into the roof of the net. First blood to the Reds!

Stung by this, the Blues surged forward. A neat one-two between Laudrup and Del Piero sent the Italian into space but Taribo West had read the situation perfectly and knocked the ball upfield to his fellow Nigerian Jay Jay Okocha. A neat flick found Michael Owen whose pace took him past a rather static Laurent Blanc. However, his crossfield pass was over-hit and the ball drifted out for a goal-kick.

The Blues were finding it hard to strike up a rhythm. Zinedine Zidane was struggling to get into the game and the much-vaunted partnership of Ronaldo and Raul had hardly seen the ball. Then Raul took a knock from an over-zealous challenge by Marcel Desailly and was replaced by Chilean striker Marcelo Salas. And that move almost immediately paid dividends.

Roberto Carlos picked up a long throw from Chilavert and surged down the left flank. He then fed Laudrup, whose first-time pass found Ronaldo on the edge of the Reds box with his back to goal and closely marked by Fabio Cannavaro. All those expecting some Brazilian magic were not to be disappointed when he scored one of the most fabulous goals this stadium has ever seen.

Two instinctive touches from thigh to knee and a lightning quick turn saw the ball scream into the postage stamp corner of Schmeichel's goal. Now the fans were treated to a non-stop feast of football, with both sides committed to all-out attack. A lung-bursting run by Michael Owen leaving three defenders in his wake was brought to a halt by a brave dive from Chilavert. Then Ronaldo's cross was met by Del Piero but his header cannoned off the bar. The clearance was completed by Lizarazu.

Half-time approached with the score remaining at one-all, but the two minutes' injury time signalled by assistant referee Paul Durkin were to prove disastrous for the Blues. Laurent Blanc dithered on a Tony Adams pass and was robbed by Bergkamp. He drew Chilavert and knocked it across for Michael Owen. The eighteen-year-old striker tapped in the easiest goal of his career. Two-one to the Reds.

The second half commenced with Oliver Bierhoff replacing Bergkamp and Dragan Stojkovic taking over from the hugely-disappointing Zinedine Zidane.

Stojkovic was eager to impress, and within five minutes of the restart nearly levelled the scores. A brilliant run from deep within his own half saw him unleash a 25-yard screamer. But he was reckoning without the agility of Peter Schmeichel in the Reds' goal. The giant Dane threw himself across the goal to finger-tip the ball round the post. Tony Adams came up for the resulting corner but his far-post header drifted wide.

This was the signal for some concerted pressure on the Reds' goal. A Thierry Henry volley was parried by Schmeichel, and only a last-gasp tackle by Cannavaro stopped Ronaldo from scoring his second goal.

It was one-way traffic to Schmeichel's goal and only the occasional breakaway by Owen or Overmars brought any respite. The Blues' manager Mario Zagallo threw caution to the wind and he brought on Davor Suker for Laurent Blanc.

Five minutes later, the Blues drew level. A brief interchange between Laudrup and Ronaldo saw the Brazilian switch the ball to the left. Roberto Carlos, on the overlap, met the ball on the volley from all of thirty yards and the ball was in the back of the net before Schmeichel could move.

Two-all and with fifteen minutes to go it was anyone's game. Both sides could easily have doubled their score. Marcelo Salas' dipping volley flashed past the post, an Overmars run was foiled by a desperate tackle by Adams and both Okocha and Stojkovic hit the bar with headers.

Then, with eighty minutes on the clock - controversy! Ronaldo's low cross into a packed goalmouth seemed to strike Denilson on the hand. Accidentally or deliberately? Referee Hugh Dallas had no doubt and pointed to the spot. Denilson and Desailly were booked for protesting and once the dust had settled, Ronaldo drilled the ball home. Three-two. Could the Reds pull this one out of the fire?

Chilavert's goal was under constant pressure as the minutes ticked away. An Overmars volley was charged down by Tony Adams and it took an amazing reaction save by the Paraguayan keeper to stop a Lizarazu effort. Owen and Bierhoff both had chances but it was left to a ginger-haired Nigerian to have the last laugh.

A jinking run by Ortega was foiled by a firm challenge by Thuram. The ball broke to Okocha who killed the ball, looked up, and curled a beauty in at Chilavert's far post. Three-all.

A truly memorable game played by two memorable sides. Wonder what the score would have been had they REALLY played!

Match statistics:
Blues 3 (Ronaldo 33,80 (pen).
R. Carlos 57).
Reds 3 (Bergkamp 15, Owen 45,
Okocha 88)

lookin ahead...

● *Michael Owen*

PENALTY shoot-outs. Three words that send a shiver through every England fan. The 1990 World Cup in Italy saw Stuart Pearce and Chris Waddle miss spot-kicks as England crashed out to West Germany in the semi-finals. Gareth Southgate suffered a similar fate in Euro '96 against the Germans.

Everyone hoped for better fortune in France 98 as Glenn Hoddle's men faced Argentina in another shoot-out to decide who would advance to the quarter-finals.

An expectant nation was left to weep again, however, as Paul Ince and David Batty joined the ever-growing list of players who will be forever remembered for missing vital penalties.

Of all the sudden-death defeats, this was a particularly hard one to take. England deserved better after defending heroically for over an hour with 10 men following the dismissal of David Beckham.

There was no shame in defeat.

Once again, luck deserted England at the crucial moment. But that has strengthened Hoddle's hand as he attempts to guide the country to the 2000 European Championship Finals, hosted jointly by Holland and Belgium. The whole country is behind him as he goes in search of glory.

The majority of the players that did the country so proud in France are good enough and young enough to be able put the record straight. There is no need for wholesale changes.

The World Cup not only confirmed the team's place amongst the world's elite, it also helped the development of the younger members of the squad. Five of the team that faced Argentina were 23 or under, with six others under 30 on the bench.

The player who profited most was Michael Owen. The Liverpool youngster was one of the stars of the tournament.

With just one season of Premiership football behind him, many believed he was going to France to make up the numbers. He had other ideas.

Whether by luck or design, Hoddle could hold him back no

● *Gary Neville*

longer. The 18-year-old rewarded his coach by making the best defences in the world quake with fear. His wonder goal against Argentina, arguably the best of the tournament, was the icing on the cake.

His partnership with Alan Shearer is one of the best in world football - and it will continue to be so for many years.

Elsewhere, Paul Scholes acquitted himself admirably in his first taste of international tournament football, Gary Neville and Sol Campbell proved themselves to be world-class defenders, and

● *Paul Scholes scores against Tunisia.*

Rio Ferdinand gained useful squad experience.

Equally encouraging is the list of talented young players Hoddle left behind. Phil Neville will surely become an established internationalist alongside his brother, while Jamie Redknapp and Robbie Fowler will be desperate to force their way back into Hoddle's plans after injuries robbed them of the chance of going to the World Cup.

So, England left France down but by no means out. Even the harshest of critics would have to concede that they have a great chance of winning the European Championships - as long as they can avoid those infuriating penalty shoot-outs!

But long before England can be installed as favourites for Euro 2000, they have to negotiate a tricky qualifying group. Luxembourg should be comparatively easy, but Hoddle's men face hazardous trips to Bulgaria, Sweden and Poland. Poland were disposed of home and away when qualifying for France 98, but although Sweden failed to reach the Finals and Bulgaria were a disappointment, they are sure to provide a strong test for England.

WHILE JOHN COLLINS, Colin Hendry and Co. were firmly in the spotlight during Scotland's brief involvement in the World Cup Finals, Kieran McAnespie went almost unnoticed in the background.

Taken along just for the experience as the Scots warmed up in the USA and then failed once more to get beyond the first round, McAnespie spent his first foray into the big time running errands and cleaning the superstars' boots.

But the St. Johnstone starlet could be one of the main men by the time Craig Brown takes his team back on the road towards Euro 2000 - and boss Brown admits he may well have to find another gofer to do the dirty work in Belgium and Holland!

"Kieran is exactly the type of young player I hope will break through in time for the next European Championships," admits the Scotland coach.

"So far, he hasn't had too many first-team games for his club, but now St. Johnstone have lost Leigh Jenkinson, I expect him to force his way in.

"No-one outside of Perth really knows him yet, but he is a left-sided midfielder with a great future, and he showed in the States and in France that he is keen as mustard.

"It's not everyone's cup of tea, cleaning the players' boots, collecting the dirty kit for the laundry basket, setting up the training pitches and so on.

"But Kieran was always eager to be involved, and he'll have learned a lot from seeing the established men at work."

Brown's enthusiasm, however, is based on more than blind optimism. For, while Kieran may have had precious few first-team outings at McDiarmid Park, he has already shown that he will grab a chance if he gets one.

And while playing in a high school stadium in front of 200 fans might only sound comparable to reserve team football in Perth, it provided Kieran with the perfect opportunity to win over his international boss.

"While I was with the squad in the USA, a match was arranged against local side the New York/New Jersey MetroStars," recalls the 18-year-old, who has already played for his country at Under-21 level.

"I was doing my usual thing, carrying the kit and the half-time juice, when the gaffer decided to give me a chance.

"He put me on in place of Darren Jackson, I managed to get a goal, and we went on to win 4-0. There may not have been thousands of spectators there to see it, but it was the most important goal I've ever scored.

"Now I have to get into the Saints side and stay there - then who knows? Maybe somebody will be cleaning MY boots by Euro 2000!"

Scotland's qualifying group for Euro 2000 consists of the Czech Republic, Lithuania, Bosnia-Herzegovina, the Faroe Islands and Estonia. What, after the non-event during World Cup qualification, are the chances of actually playing in Estonia this time?! ∎

● *Kieran McAnespie*

wish you

When Dundee's David and Pauline Kelly and their so[...]
World Cup last summer, we asked them to send us a[...]

➤ Here's the map. We turn left at Dover...easy!

➤ Paris...and Jamie has his first look at the Stade de France.

➤ Bordeaux, but no tickets for the Norway match. Plenty atmosphere outside the ground at the big screen.

➤ Time for sight-seeing

➤ YEE-SS! We HAVE tickets for the Morocco match. Pauline and Jamie proudly show off their precious tickets.

➤ Pity a[...]

were here!

...amie, nine, travelled to follow Scotland's progress in the
...postcard. Better still, they sent us some photographs!

➤ Mixing with Brazil fans...a Scottish samba!

➤ From Paris to Bordeaux via Orleans and
its "Dundee Pub".

...tiful village of St. Emilion.

➤ What's better? A hotel...

...or a campsite?!

...esult!

➤ Heading for home via Euro Disney and
...lanet Hollywood.

■ The Kellys are all members of
the Scotland Travel Club, and
look forward
to Euro 2000.
Will Scotland
qualify? Of
course we
will, they say!
Better start
saving!

THE SCOTTISH FOOTBALL ASSOCIATION

fully booked!

Referee URIAH RENNIE is in great demand!

RIAH RENNIE is one of the country's most recognised and respected referees. The 38-year-old Sheffield whistler is the first black official to referee in the Premiership and his performances in the middle have earned him a reputation for being one of the most commanding 'law enforcers' in the game.

Despite only making his debut on the Premiership list of referees last season, he is very much in demand. Regarded as one of the rising stars, there is hardly a free date in his diary. He is a regular speaker at sports functions up and down the country and is also on the Football Task Force.

Away from football, he works as a manager at a Sheffield leisure centre and, when he can fit it in, is also a local magistrate.

Add to that exhausting list the fact that Uriah is also a doting dad and it is hard to believe he has any time left over to referee some of the biggest matches in the Premiership.

Many referees pick up the whistle because their own playing career has been cut short through injury or because they could not make the grade as a player, but that was not the case with Rennie. He showed promise as a young player, but chose to forsake any hopes of a professional career to concentrate on his academic studies. He has a degree in Physical Education and a masters degree in Business Administration.

"I don't consider myself a frustrated footballer, although I would have liked to play the game like the great Brazilian players of the 1980s, Socrates and Zico.

"I played for an amateur side in Sheffield in my younger days and they wanted me to have a trial for Corby Town, who were then a nursery club for Northampton Town. But I wanted to concentrate on my academic studies and only saw sport as something to enjoy and not to make a living from.

"My route into refereeing was through the Physical Education background. By the time I got the local kids organised on a Saturday in the winter there was not time for me to play the game. I took my referee's FA Prelim badge instead.

"I qualified as a referee in 1979 and made it on to the Grade 1 list in 1984. I was promoted to the Northern Premier Middle in 1986 and worked my way through the ranks until I finally reached the Referees Panel in 1990 before making the full referees list in 1994. I made my debut on the Premiership list last season."

Uriah has been a big success officiating Premiership matches. His common-sense approach has helped him gain the respect of players, managers and spectators. He is able to keep up with play thanks to a rigorous and unusual training regime that includes kick-boxing, trampolining and marathon running.

"Fitness should be an integral part of any referee's job description," he further adds. "The true test of a good referee is to have a rounded ability. That is the experience to anticipate where incidents will occur and the athletic ability to be there when it happens.

"As for my varied sporting activities, I don't want to be one-dimensional. I try to do things that I am not good at. It helps to break up my training and keep it interesting."

Uriah has stacked up an impressive list of sporting achievements. He has played indoor hockey at international level and lacrosse at county level. His sporting prowess has even gained him entry to the prestigious Guinness Book of Records.

He explains, "I play a lot of rounders. When Sheffield Polytechnic did a study on human performance and projectile games a few years ago I was filmed throwing underarm a rounders ball. My speed was clocked at 68mph, which makes me the fastest rounders bowler in the world.

"Working at a leisure centre also gives you a rare insight into how

> **"I don't like being in the spotlight, but I have a certain responsibility."**

sportsmen prepare and compete. Where I work I meet people from a variety of sporting backgrounds, for instance water polo, volleyball and badminton. There is always something I can incorporate from them into my sporting discipline."

But while Uriah's progress through the ranks appears to have been swift and smooth, he reveals that he has had his share of mishaps along the way.

And nothing could have prepared him for a baptism of fire on his debut as a Football League referee in 1994.

Uriah continues, "I made my debut on August 13, 1994, at Feethams, Darlington. Preston North End were the visitors but they encountered heavy traffic and arrived late at the ground. I had to put the kick-off back 26 minutes.

"Later, when I arrived home there were loads of messages on my answering machine from friends who had seen a heading on teletext which read 'Chaos at Feethams.'

"They thought I had been too keen on showing yellow and red cards. Ironically, I did register the first booking of the new season that day. I cautioned a player after only four seconds.

"The first season was a difficult one for me. There were a lot of rule changes following the World Cup in the United States. The learning curve was steeper than I imagined and with all the new law amendments I went into a new environment with a new style and a lack of experience.

"I consider myself a conciliatory referee, but I found that in the early years on the Football League list I was cautioning a lot. I've found a happy balance in recent years."

Uriah is reluctant to step into the spotlight, but admits that as a role model he has no choice.

"I don't like being in the spotlight, but as the first black referee in the Premiership, I have a certain responsibility," he adds. "I try to encourage black and Asian referees to come through the ranks. I get a lot of correspondence. Some of it is from people who are just pleased to see a black referee on television. I also get letters and phone calls from organisations and also academics who are doing research into how a black person gets on in a white dominated environment.

"I know I am recognised by a lot of people because I am black. If I was white it might be a different story.

"My advice is that there are barriers for minorities, but they can be broken down. It is important to get this across. At the moment, if I was to leave Grade 1 there would be a void. There are a couple of black referees coming through but it will take three or four years. It is crucial that they have the appropriate experience and ability.

"But there are many positive aspects to it as well. Last year, I refereed in the West Indies for 17 days and played a part in trying to get a professional football league up and running in Trinidad and Tobago. I would not have been able to do that if I was not black." ■

● *And if anyone wants to take up refereeing, Uriah urges them to contact the Football Association, 16 Lancaster Gate, London W2 3LW.*
Phone 0171 262 4542

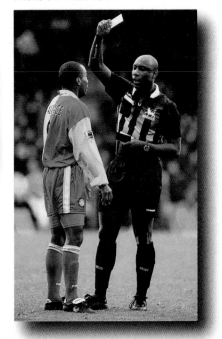

feeling blue

Despite a bad start, LORENZO AMORUSO loves life with Rangers

rANGERS' ITALIAN import Lorenzo Amoruso is loving every minute of his time at Ibrox because, at last, he is able to show the fans what he is capable of. The man brought in to replace former fans' favourite, Richard Gough, is finally doing his talking on the park, after a nightmare first term in Glasgow.

Following his £4million move from Fiorentina, the 27-year-old managed to clock up just six appearances for Walter Smith's men, suffering on the sidelines for much of what turned out to be a very disappointing League campaign.

There was also the heartache

of missing out on the Scottish Cup to leave the Ibrox side without a single trophy to show for their efforts. But now Lorenzo is feeling fitter than ever and is ready to bring new honours to Ibrox.

"I love it at Rangers," enthuses the former Serie A star. "I already have very strong feelings for this club after being here just a short time.

"I would not have signed a four-year contract if I hadn't wanted to be a part of Rangers' success and, after missing out on lifting a trophy last season, I am very keen to make up for what

> **"I am very keen to make up for what was a very disappointing time for me."**

was a very disappointing time for me.

"Being out of action for so long was very hard to take, but I played in a few big games when I returned and that gave me the chance to start showing people what I can do.

"The first two matches I played for Rangers were both against Celtic and we won both of them, which really helped me get back into my stride. Now that we will be trying to get the Championship back from Parkhead, I hope that trend will continue."

After that Old Firm double

Amoruso is unable to prevent Stephane Adam from sealing Hearts' Scottish Cup victory by scoring the Edinburgh club's second goal.

bill, Lorenzo then found himself in the thick of the action in the Scottish Cup Final against one of his best friends in football, Hearts' Stefano Salvatori.

"I know Stefano very well and when I first came to Scotland I travelled through to Edinburgh to visit him and he helped me to settle in quickly.

"But I've also been helped by the amazing atmosphere here at Ibrox.

"The whole team just feels like one big family and I think that is very important. The new coach, Dick Advocaat, will have to make sure that he keeps that atmosphere at the club, because it really makes a very big difference to the team.

"When I signed for Rangers, I told David Murray that I wanted to win with him and his club and I still feel very much that way. I've had a winning philosophy throughout my career and it isn't about to change.

"It is going to become more and more difficult for us to pick up trophies, but I am a very confident player and I have every confidence in my team." ■

side-tracked!

League business is the No.1 priority for Middlesbrough's MARK SCHWARZER!

GOALKEEPER Mark Schwarzer has crammed enough highs and lows into his brief Boro career to last a lifetime. The 26-year-old Australian has seen the Riverside outfit relegated and promoted in the two seasons he has been there. They have also been to three cup finals, losing them all.

But Schwarzer's career has always featured the unexpected. It has been one big emotional roller-coaster ride.

After showing early promise at German side Kaislerslautern, he fell out of favour and returned from an international match to find he was relegated to third choice.

Soon afterwards, he was snapped up by First Division Bradford City, who then sold him on to Boro for £1.5m after just a handful of games.

Some impressive performances suggested he could help the Teesiders out of a hole. They were fighting for their Premiership lives. But with a couple of months of the season remaining he suffered a broken leg and was out of action for six months. He missed two cup finals and watched from the sidelines as his side were relegated on the final day of the season.

He returned last season to star in Boro's glorious promotion campaign, although he tasted defeat in the Coca-Cola Cup Final at the hands of Chelsea.

"Returning to the Premiership at the first time of asking was a great achievement, but that is where we feel we belong.

"As for our spate of cup final defeats, some clubs don't make any cup finals at all, but here we chalked up a hat-trick and that is a tremendous achievement, especially when you consider we were a First Division side last season."

Despite winning promotion last term, Schwarzer believed he was playing better the previous season before he suffered a broken leg and the side were relegated.

"I know what I can do and I am very self-critical," he adds.

"Some people have said to me, 'There was nothing wrong with your game,' but I know there were parts of my game, which I normally excel in, which suffered because of lapses of confidence. "My form was not as good as it was the previous season. I would say that I was performing at about 15 per cent less than my best. That might not sound much, but it was to me. Thankfully, winning promotion put it to the back of my mind."

Schwarzer stresses that Boro will be mindful of avoiding the pitfalls that cost them their Premiership status two seasons ago.

They were on course to avoid the drop, but got involved in the latter stages of the Coca-Cola Cup and FA Cup. The heavy toll of games eventually cost them dear.

In particular, Schwarzer is sure that the defeat by Leicester City in the Coca-Cola Cup Final replay was the start of the rot setting in.

"I have always believed that if we had won the Coca-Cola Cup at the first time of asking, we would not have been relegated," he goes on.

"Leicester equalised with just two minutes to play. The confidence in the players just drained away after that. We were so near to the club's first major honour, only to let it slip through our fingers.

"The statistics back me up in this belief. Prior to Christmas, we lost 13 consecutive games, but we were the form team in the New Year. However, after drawing at Wembley we hardly won a match.

"We have talked about that day as a turning point in our season. Although we had a marvellous day out at Wembley and we didn't lose the match, a lot of the guys in the dressing room agree that it turned out to be a black day for the club.

"We cannot afford to let cup football distract us from our main aim. And that is to ensure that we don't lose our prized Premiership status again!" ∎

CROSSword

See 39 across

across

6. Swedish striker Henrik (7)
7. This David is one of Fergie's young stars (7)
9. Part of the body that cannot control the ball...unless you're a goalkeeper (3)
10. England's 1998 Double winners (7)
11. Brazilian legend from the 1960s (4)
12. Pull or grab back unfairly (4)
15. Middlesbrough's Robbie (6)
17. Leicester striker Emile (6)
18. Evening fixture, a — match (5)
20. Coventry or Leicester (4)
23. Two of Jason McAteer's clubs (9, 6)
25. Redfearn, Sullivan or Shipperley (4)
26. Messrs Winterburn and Martyn (5)
28. Spurs keeper Ian (6)
30. Start of the season game, the Charity — (6)
31. West Ham are in this End of London (4)
33. Ex-Liverpool legend, striker Ian (4)
35. Supporters' flags (7)
36. Villa defender Ehiogu (3)
38. The man with the whistle (7)
39. Celtic's Paul, ex-Borussia Dortmund (7)

down

1. Spanish city with a Real team (6)
2. Group of directors who run a club (5)
3. Awarded for a foul in the box (7)
4. TV company with sports channels (3)
5. Championship-winning manager of Liverpool and Blackburn (8)
8. Roy Keane's international team (8, 2, 7)
11. Arsenal's French midfielder Emmanuel (5)
13. Player not in the first team (7)
14. John who followed Brian Little as Villa boss (7)
16. Bobby or Jack (8)
19. These Rovers play in Birkenhead (8)
21. Fulham's home, Craven — (7)
22. Hits the ball into the net (7)
24. Describes a player from Ryan Giggs' country (5)
27. These keep a player out of the game (8)
29. Sea-faring nickname of Bristol Rovers (7)
32. Hull's nickname (6)
34. Middlesbrough boss Mr Robson (5)
37. Millwall's ground, the New —(3)

answers

fish hooked!

Why MARK FISH preferred Bolton to Bologna!

WHEN defender Mark Fish joined his team-mates in the South African international squad in France last summer, he regarded the occasion as more than just an opportunity to enjoy the high point of his career so far.

The 25-year-old defender viewed the World Cup Finals as a chance to strengthen further the bonds which have tied together the peoples of South Africa.

Fish and his countrymen have been revelling in the rebirth of their nation, and he believes that football has played an important part in that process.

"When we went to France, we were aware that the eyes of the world were on South Africa," he says. "It was vital to continue the momentum which we started when we won the African Nations Cup in 1996. During that success, we united our country.

"What we did for South Africa then was more important to the players than the money we earned for winning the tournament or collecting the trophy at the end of it.

"Before then, the white population would have been familiar with the names of all our rugby and cricket players, but wouldn't have known the soccer players. Now they know all about players like Doctor Khumalo and John 'Shoes' Moshoeu.

"People of every colour, creed and nation started supporting South Africa during the three to four weeks of the tournament and, ever since, the support has been growing and growing.

"Considering the defeat which the Springboks rugby team suffered at the hands of the British Lions in 1997, it is our football team which has done really well in world sport during the last year or so."

The focus of most of Fish's attention during his first season in English football was on Bolton Wanderers' battle against relegation from the Premiership.

Had he taken a gamble a year before joining the Lancashire club, however, he might have found himself going for glory in the Championship and the European Cup.

Back in 1996, he turned down an opportunity to impress Manchester United. Instead of moving to Old Trafford, he spent a year in the Italian Serie A, playing for Lazio.

"A lot of people still ask me, 'How could you have turned down Manchester United?' In fact, I didn't," Mark points out.

"When I left South Africa after our success in the African Nations Cup, I had an agreement with both Lazio and Manchester United that I would go to see both clubs.

"I arrived in Manchester first and watched United play in a match against Everton. Manager Alex Ferguson said he liked the way I played, but wanted me to stay for a two-week trial.

"Since I had been a United fan as a boy, I was a little bit disappointed that Mr Ferguson had offered me a chance to come to Manchester, then asked me to stay for an extended trial.

"I didn't say no, but explained that I also had an obligation to speak to Lazio. When I did so, they wanted me to sign straight away.

"When I made my decision to join Lazio, it was my head ruling my heart. To me, the Italian League was still the best in the world, so I was satisfied with my choice. It would have been a dream to play for United, but I was realising another by playing in Serie A.

"I believe that what I learned in Italy, I couldn't have learned elsewhere. They have the best defences in the world. My way of defending and my tactical play improved immensely while I was with Lazio.

"But it was off the field where they made me a better player and a better person.

"I had my wild days back in South Africa, but the Italians knocked that out of me and instilled a much more responsible attitude into me.

"In South Africa, I played for Orlando Pirates, the biggest club in the country. In my first year with them, we won the League, the first time the club had won the Championship for 27 years.

"However, I was reckless in the

way that I lived. My life at that time was just one round of parties.

"Where my football career was concerned, I just took my talent for granted and spent as little time as possible working on my game.

"When I trained with the rest of the team, I couldn't wait to get off the field at the end of the session so that I could go off enjoying myself. It was the same on Saturdays after a match.

" When I went to Lazio, that all changed. In Italy, players are simply not allowed to go out drinking with the lads. It is not the Italian way, in any case.

"They are very strict about how their players live and work. I became much more professional and dedicated to football than I had ever been before.

"The parties and late nights stopped. By the time I arrived in England to play for Bolton, I had become a much more responsible person.

"I married my wife, Louie, at the start of last season and that has also helped me to settle down. I spend my spare time doing less boisterous things, like writing articles for magazines and newspapers back home in South Africa, where the public are very keen to keep track of how their players are doing abroad.

"English football is now well covered by television at home, so I have been getting some good exposure.

"It has been an enjoyable first year

for me. Most importantly, I have found the football in the Premiership tough and very challenging.

"When I arrived, I regarded it as one of the best leagues in the world. Though I felt Italy was still top, I quickly realised that English domestic football was rapidly catching up.

"The import of so many top stars and coaches has contributed to a rapid development of football in this country.

"So much so, that I believe the Premiership is now the best in the world."

Fish moved to England partly because of the number of foreigners at Lazio who were restricting his first-team opportunities.

However, he admits that the attraction of playing for Bolton manager, Colin Todd, was also a big attraction.

He goes on, "I had five Italian clubs chasing me including Bologna, but I had decided that, if I couldn't play for Lazio, I would rather not go to one of their rivals.

"They had been loyal to me and I wanted to return some of that. My initial reason for leaving was simply

because there were seven non-Italians battling for three places in the first team.

"Because the two strikers, Jugovic and Boksic, were more or less guaranteed a place, it meant there were five of us fighting for one jersey, and I didn't feel it was worth it.

"Lazio said they didn't want me to go, but I didn't like those odds. Though I had really enjoyed my spell with them, and felt I had done very well during my only full season in Italy, my thoughts turned towards England.

"When I was told about Bolton's interest, I was immediately attracted, because I already knew of Colin Todd and had been aware that he was a great player in his day.

"In South Africa, we have a

sporting hero called Andre Joubert, who played for the Springboks and has been described in rugby circles as the Rolls Royce of full-backs.

"Well, somebody told me that Colin Todd had been the Rolls Royce of centre-backs, so when Bolton enquired about me my interest was sparked. I like playing for coaches who have been good players.

"When I spoke to him, saw the Reebok Stadium and he described the attack-minded way in which he wanted his team to play, it finalised my decision to come here.

"But I would not like to say that I have finished with Italian football altogether. I enjoyed my spell there very much and would love to go back there one day and finish my career in Italy." ■

spencer prior
leicester city

christian dailly
derby county

generatio
game

STEPHEN CLEMENCE

always knew he had a lot to live up to as a professional footballer. When your dad has won 61 England caps, five Championship medals, two FA Cup and one League Cup winner's medals, three European Cup and two UEFA Cup winner's medals, it is a tough act to follow. The dad in question is former Liverpool and Tottenham goalkeeping great, Ray Clemence, who was part of England's coaching staff at the World Cup.

Stephen Clemence at least has one advantage when it comes to comparisons. He is not a goalkeeper like his dad. He got his break at Tottenham last season as a midfield player.

It all started with a dream debut against Manchester United on the opening day of the season and ended in dramatic circumstances in an FA Cup tie at Barnsley in February. That night at Oakwell is an occasion he'd rather forget. Having already been booked, Stephen was shown a second yellow card when the referee accused him of diving.

His team-mates were incensed and let the referee know exactly what they thought of him. But Stephen, showing maturity beyond his years, ran straight off, knowing the referee wouldn't change his mind.

"There was no point in

It is not easy following a famous father into the game. Everybody constantly makes the comparison — "He's not as good as his old man." Several top managers have sons playing professionally — Alex Ferguson (Darren), Harry Redknapp (Jamie), Gordon Strachan (Gavin), Colin Todd (Andy) and Kenny Dalglish (Paul).

And there are two men who, although not managers, are still heavily involved in football at its highest level. The Topical Times spoke to their sons, to find out what it's like following in a famous father's footsteps!

hanging around," says Stephen. "I could tell what the referee was going to do as soon as I picked myself up off the floor.

"That doesn't mean I accepted his decision. I've never taken a dive in my life and I certainly didn't that night.

"I don't cheat on people. Anybody who knows me will tell you that.

"That was the first time I'd been sent off in my career. It wasn't a nice experience, I can tell you. What made it worse was that my mum and dad were in the crowd that night. I felt worse for them than I did for myself.

"Dad was great about it afterwards. He was very encouraging, as he always has been.

"He's always told me the truth about myself and my football. That's the best way to be in this game. I can't have a better example to follow than dad. He achieved so much in the game

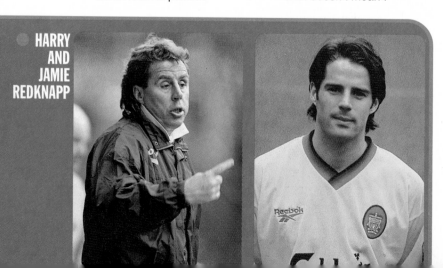

HARRY AND JAMIE REDKNAPP

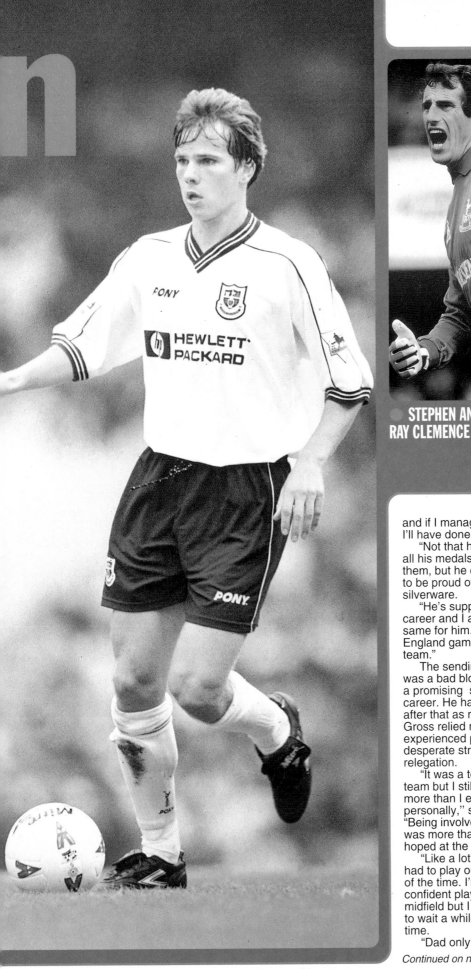

STEPHEN AND RAY CLEMENCE

and if I manage a fraction of that I'll have done well.

"Not that he's one to bring out all his medals and boast about them, but he certainly has plenty to be proud of when it comes to silverware.

"He's supported me in my career and I always try to do the same for him. I love going to England games to cheer on the team."

The sending-off at Barnsley was a bad blow to Stephen after a promising start to his first-team career. He hardly figured again after that as manager Christian Gross relied more on the experienced players in the desperate struggle against relegation.

"It was a tough season for the team but I still achieved a lot more than I expected personally," says Stephen. "Being involved in 20-odd games was more than I would ever have hoped at the start of the year.

"Like a lot of young players, I had to play out of position much of the time. I'm a much more confident player in the centre of midfield but I know I might have to wait a while to play there full time.

"Dad only had one position he

Continued on next page

could play. At least I can switch around if it means I get a game.

"It wasn't a great year at Tottenham but at least the fans were able to see David Ginola every week. He's by far the best player I've ever played with. You should see some of the things he does in training. The best thing is that he also does most of them out on the pitch on a Saturday afternoon.

"He was on top form every week for us last season. It's a shame we didn't reach the same standards as a team." ■

GAVIN AND GORDON STRACHAN

FRANK LAMPARD

It's tough enough being the son of a famous father. But it must be even tougher when the two men you are trying most to impress are your dad and your uncle.

That's the problem which 20-year-old West Ham midfielder Frank Lampard has had to conquer at Upton Park in the last couple of years. His dad, Frank senior, a former England international defender, is coach and his uncle, Harry Redknapp, is manager.

Young Frank had to battle to convince sceptical fans at Upton Park that he was in the Hammers team on merit, not because of his name. But at the same time he had to work harder than any other player to prove to the coach and manager that he was worth that first-team spot.

"People use the word nepotism. But if anything, it's been harder for young Frank because we are extra tough on him," reveals Frank senior.

"He's had to do more than anyone else to justify his place. But he's big enough to deal with it all."

Lampard played for the England Under-21 side last season, and also appeared for the B team against Chile. It may not be long before he emulates his father, who won two full caps as a left-back.

One of Frank senior's claims to fame stems from the 1980 FA Cup semi-final replay at Leeds, when West Ham beat Everton 2-1. Left-back Lampard somehow turned up in the penalty box to score the winning goal and his crazy goal celebration, involving a dance around a corner flag, became a classic.

17 years later, Frank junior returned to the Elland Road scene last season to repeat that dance, after scoring a goal for the Hammers.

"It just had to be done," said Lampard. "I'd planned to do it when I scored my first goal at home, but scoring on the same ground was too good a chance to waste."

Young Frank went on to finish the season with nine goals, a better strike rate than most Premiership midfield players. The 1998 World Cup came too soon for him, but Lampard may well figure in England's squad for the next one.

"My ambition is to play in the World Cup Finals. My target is the 2002 tournament," says Frank.

FRANK JNR AND FRANK SNR

"I've enjoyed playing for the Under-21 and B teams. Now I want to emulate my dad by winning a full cap.

"It's definitely been a big help to me to have my dad as the coach. But at the same time, he's always been my biggest critic.

"He just wants me to do better. We have arguments, but in the end I accept that he knows a lot about the game.

"When I started out in the West Ham team, I was still living with my parents. I decided to move into my own flat to give myself a bit of space.

"It means I'm not talking football all the time. I'm more relaxed. But I appreciate that I've learned a lot from my dad that other kids could never have got from their fathers. I believe I have more knowledge about the game than most lads of my age.

"I feel I have developed a lot in the last year. I've proved I can hold a first-team place on merit.

"When I first played in the team I took a lot of stick from some fans who thought I was just picked because of my dad. I knew that wasn't the case, but I had to prove it."

Frank Lampard senior, a one-club man, is second only to Billy Bonds in the all-time appearance list for West Ham. He played over 650 first-team matches.

Young Frank has a long way to go to match that record. But he is on the way. So far, the boy has done well. ■

what happened next?

■ The final seconds of an F.A. Cup Third Round tie...a corner is whipped into Wrexham's six yard box... Wimbledon's Marcus Gayle rises above everyone to head home a match-winning goal! Or did he?

TURN OVER

■ Not according to referee Steve Dunn who blew for full-time just before the ball crossed the line! Relief all round for Wrexham as the match ended nil-nil, but to say the Wimbledon players were annoyed is putting it mildly. They had the last laugh, however. Wimbledon won the replay 3-2.

flashback

■ As some readers MIGHT remember, the same thing happened in the 1978 World Cup Finals in a match between Brazil and Sweden. Brazil scored what they thought was the winner, but the Welsh referee Clive Thomas disallowed the goal because he had blown for full-time!

tore andre flo
chelsea

TTFB — First ever sighting of Ronaldo.

BR — I first saw him on TV playing for PSV Eindhoven in 1994.

TTFB — Could you then see the potential he has since realised to become the World's Number One?

BR — Absolutely! Although he was young and inexperienced, he showed the pace, strength and ability that made Barcelona fork out £13.3m for him, despite being only 18.

TTFB — Ronaldo has been compared to Pele. Is that a fair comparison?

BR — No! Not yet. He's only 22 and although his performances at club level have been outstanding, he has never shown his class in a global context, i.e. The World Cup. Ronaldo, despite one or two flashes of brilliance had a comparitively disappointing World Cup especially in the final when he looked unfit.

TTFB — Did you ever play against Pele?

BR — Unfortunately not. I played for England against Brazil in the 1958 World Cup finals , but Pele wasn't in the Brazilian line-up. He made his first appearance in the quarter-finals and by that time, England had been knocked out of the competition by Russia.

TTFB — In your career, you managed three of the world's top strikers - Gary Lineker, Ronaldo and Romario. Who, in your opinion, was the best?

BR — They were or are all great strikers, and it is impossible to single out one of them. Lineker was an instinctive goalscorer, a predator, deadly in the penalty box. Romario and Ronaldo are great dribblers - Gary wasn't. Great strikers in their own right.

TTFB — You've had success in management both at home and abroad. What are the differences between continental and domestic management?

BR — Quite simply, in continental football the manager manages the team - that's all. When I was with Ipswich I was handling the press, arranging transfers, working on the commercial side,scouting... everything. At Barcelona, the only thing I had to worry about was the team!

TTFB — Do your successes with PSV, Porto and Barcelona compare with the glory years at Ipswich?

BR — At Ipswich, I had to build the team from scratch. In fact I had to build THREE teams in the fourteen years I was there. You're in at the sharp end from the very start. At Barcelona, although I inherited an

double dutch

Holland... Portugal... Spain...

excellent squad, I still had to buy six players — like Ronaldo. Success is great no matter where you are, but sweeter with a team you've nurtured from the beginning.

TTFB — Pound for pound, who is the best signing you have made for any club?

BR — That's a difficult one. I signed some great lads at Ipswich - Muhren, Osman, Thijssen, Mariner. But if you had to push me on this one, I'd have to say Ronaldo.

TTFB — If Glenn Hoddle resigned as England coach, would you relish taking on that job again?

BR — The only way I'd move in as England coach would be as a stop-gap. I was sorry to leave after eight years, but Glenn Hoddle is doing a great job and I wish him all the best.

TTFB — Your namesake Bryan is making his mark at Middlesbrough. Being a north-east man, are you pleased to see the resurgence of clubs like Middlesbrough and Sunderland?

BR — Of course! I'm a Geordie from Durham and it's terrific to see teams from the north-east doing well. The supporters up there are passionate about their soccer and with three teams from the same area

pulling in 30,000-plus every Saturday, it has to be good for the game.

TTFB — What is your fondest memory?

BR — Another hard one! I have lots. Two stand out, though. My first cap for England v France at Wembley in 1957 and managing England in the World Cup in 1990.

TTFB — What is the best goal you've seen scored?

BR — Again it's hard to pick out just one. However, Roberto Carlos's goal in Le Tournoi for Brazil v France must be there or thereabouts. He put an unbelievable swerve on that ball. I also saw Ronaldo beat five men and score against Compostela for Barcelona. And there's John Barnes's epic for England in Rio. I kept shouting for him to hit it but he kept beating men before rolling it into the net!

TTFB — You played in the 1961 9-3 demolition of Scotland at Wembley. Is that your most memorable international appearance?

BR — Second most memorable, even though I scored the first goal that day. I'd have to go back to my

first cap. That England team contained some of the legendary Busby Babes - like Duncan Edwards.

TTFB — What was your saddest moment? The 1990 defeat by Germany? Or telling a young player his career was over?

BR — Many times I had to break the bad news to a young lad, to say that he wouldn't make the grade. The more you did it, the better you became. The World Cup semi-final defeat was hard to take, because I knew we could have gone on to beat Argentina in the Final.

TTFB — Do you have any ambitions left in soccer?

BR — I've never won the Premiership or the old First Division title. I came close with Ipswich twice, only to lose out both times on the last day of the season. I've also never won the World Cup. These would be nice ways to end my career!

TTFB — One last question. Is there any youngster you could tip for the top?

BR — One young lad, the Argentinian Juan Roman Riquelme. He plays for Boca Juniors and he's dynamite - and only 19! ∎

and back to Holland

Dennis Bergkamp, Arsenal, and David Wetherall, Leeds.

Tore André Flo, Norway

high
kicking

Chris Sutton, Blackburn Rovers.

Carlos Gamarra, Paraguay.

andy hinchcliffe
sheffield wednesday

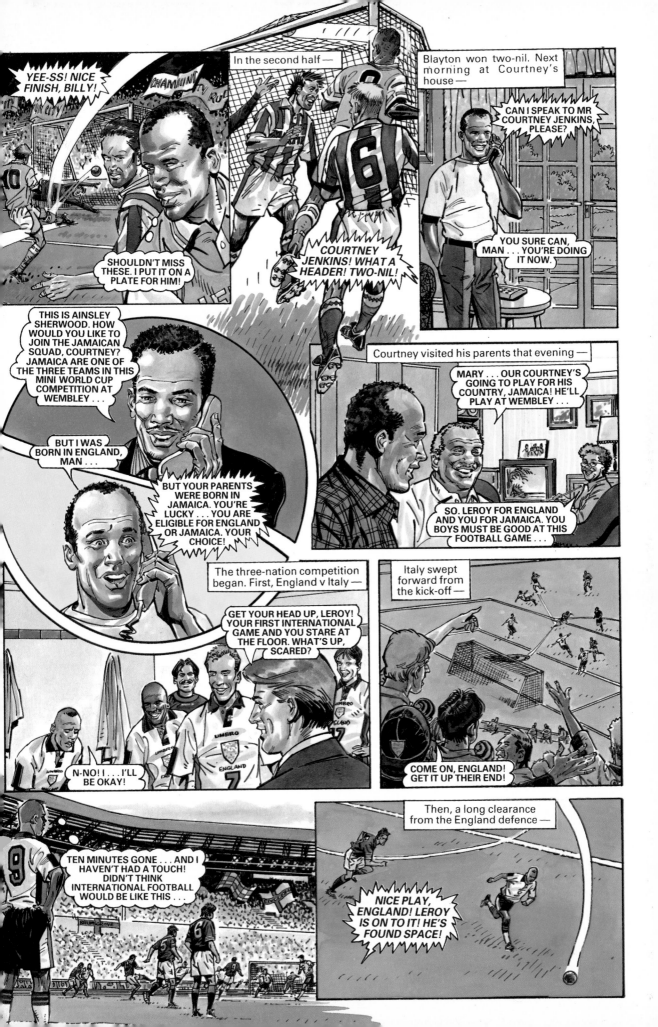

gareth southgate

aston villa

chris sutton
blackburn rovers

sweet and sour!

CLIVE MENDONCA — the hat-trick hero and villain!

T was the best of times... it was the worst of times. Scoring a hat-trick at Wembley and helping your team win promotion to the Premiership in the process would be a dream come true for any player. For Clive Mendonca that joy also brought heartache.

The Charlton hot-shot scored three brilliant goals in last season's amazing Division One play-off final, which finished up 4-4 after extra-time. He then tucked away the first spot-kick as Charlton won the high-tension penalty shoot-out 7-6.

Cue celebrations in South-East London.

The only problem for Mendonca was that Charlton's vanquished opponents on that memorable afternoon in May were Sunderland, the team he'd supported since he was a boy. If only they'd both been promoted, he'd have had the best of both worlds.

"To score a hat-trick at Wembley was unbelievable,'' says Clive. ''But I still felt gutted for Sunderland after the match.

"Although I was born in London, I moved to Sunderland when I was only two years old and stayed there until I was sixteen. They were always my team and I'm the biggest Sunderland fan in the world.

"A professional footballer has to do his job and for me that means scoring goals for Charlton. I'd had a very strong feeling I was going to score that day at Wembley, but I didn't expect to get three.

"It was very sad that such a great day had to finish with one player missing a penalty. Michael Gray went to the same school as I did in Sunderland so I really felt for him when that happened.

"You wouldn't believe how much pressure there

Clive's goals v. Sunderland. One...two...and three.

is on a player when he steps up to take his turn in a penalty shoot-out. The whole world seems to be watching you at the time. It's very tough on the player who eventually misses. Michael was the unlucky one that day."

Wembley marked the end of what had been an incredible first season for Clive at Charlton. Signed for a club record £700,000, he scored 26 league goals to take the team right to the brink of automatic promotion.

"I always think I'm going to score goals," says Clive. "If my team-mates create the chances, I'll stick them

away.

"I've always been a 20-a-season man throughout my career. The great challenge is to do that again this year in

the highest division of the lot.

"Last season in Division One was tough enough with some very good teams like Nottingham Forest, Middlesbrough and Sunderland scrapping it out for promotion. In the end it was a great shame that both Sunderland and ourselves couldn't go up because we both had more than enough points to deserve it.

"That was the thing about last season. The top teams just couldn't stop winning. We had a tremendous unbeaten run at the end of the campaign but it still wasn't enough to get us up automatically.

"If we thought that was tough, the Premiership is something else again. The quality there these days is unbelievable.

"When I was at Sheffield United I did play in the old Division One and ever since then I've been desperate to play at the highest level again. The Premiership is the only place to test yourself as a player." ∎

■ Kevin Pressman (Shefield Wednesday) tussles with Stuart Pearce (Newcastle United)

■ Pegguy Arphexad (Leicester City) foils Sol Campbell (Spurs)

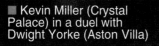

■ Kevin Miller (Crystal Palace) in a duel with Dwight Yorke (Aston Villa)

safe**keep**

Being a goalie can be tough!

■ Tim Flowers (Blackburn Rovers) faces an aerial threat from Arsenal's Ian Wright.

Sheffield Wednesday's Matt Clarke battles it out with team-mates and opponents alike in a match against Coventry City.

ping?

The "Topical Times" spoke to GRAEME LE SAUX about Chelsea's United Nations!

globetr

yOU could pick a great World XI from the stars on show at Stamford Bridge. Italy, Norway, Russia, Wales, Scotland, Romania, France, Nigeria, Uruguay, Jamaica, Holland and England... top footballers have come from all over the world to play for Chelsea in the last couple of years.

England's Graeme Le Saux loves that lively mix in the Chelsea dressing-room. The man from Jersey feels perfectly at home in Gianluca Vialli's cosmopolitan gang.

In such company, a foreign language wouldn't go amiss. And Le Saux proved he could speak French for a BBC advert shown before the World Cup, also starring Les Ferdinand, Martin Keown and Ally McCoist.

Unfortunately, Le Saux has to admit his French isn't actually that good despite being born only a short boat trip away from the coast of France.

"Some of the foreign lads at Chelsea can speak three or four different languages,'' says Le Saux. "But people who know me will tell you that my French isn't up to much.

"Wherever the players come from, we all try to speak the same language on the pitch at Chelsea. This is a very exciting place to play football alongside so many top international stars.

"The chance to line up with Gianfranco Zola and Roberto di Matteo was one of the big attractions when I returned to Chelsea at the start of last season. It was very different to when I first started at the club as a youngster.

"It wasn't long before I found myself going head-to-head with Gianfranco

Zola in the crucial World Cup qualifier against Italy in Rome. We'd quickly become good friends but there was more than a little banter between us in the build-up to that particular game.

"He said to me, 'Two weeks before the game I won't speak to you, a week before the game I start kicking you'. We had to laugh about the whole situation.

"That's life at Chelsea. There's always somebody off playing an international somewhere and it might well be against another Chelsea player.

"I got on with our Italian

contingent straightaway after joining Chelsea. They're just such great guys.

"Roberto Di Matteo and myself would ring each other up in different parts of Europe to wish each other luck before big games. We might have been international rivals, but that didn't stop us being friends.

"When you see a player for the first time you might admire him from a professional point of view. But if you're going to be in the same team, you want to be his friend too.

"Franco Zola always used to carry his phrasebook around so he'd be able to find the

right words. Usually so he could be cheeky to a team-mate.

"He really is a great personality. Couple that with his natural ability and you get a very rounded person.

"There are no airs and graces about Franco. He's always there doing extra work in training.

"He loves playing football in England. There's much less pressure on him than there was in Italy, believe it or not.

"Franco is just one of the great international stars who have been gracing Stamford Bridge over the last few years. The squad has had so many different cultures and contrasting personalities.

"The important thing is that Ruud Gullit and then Gianluca Vialli gelled those wonderful foreign players and some excellent home-grown talent into a great team that did well both domestically and in Europe.

"If you're playing with players with similar attitude and ideas on the pitch, then everybody understands what they're supposed to do. It doesn't matter what language you speak when you're playing football.

"That's why the rotation system has worked so well at Chelsea over the last year or so. We've always had players who can come in and do the same job as the player they're replacing.

"It's a great position to be in as a team. Gianluca Vialli takes one international striker off and he puts another one on in his place — sometimes himself."

Le Saux has proved himself one of the best left-backs in the Premiership over the last few years and England's top man in the

> **"Wherever the players come from, we all try to speak the same language on the pitch at Chelsea."**

otters!

position as well. He's also shown himself to be one of the game's great competitors, which sometimes gets him into trouble.

"There's this transformation that takes place before a match," says Le Saux. "I become fiercely competitive and desperate to win.

"There are times when I get frustrated and I know it shows on my face. Hopefully, as I get older I will be able to control it better.

"These days there's so much analysis of what happens on the pitch. When you're an England player, people are watching every move you make.

"I could make a genuine attempt to make a fair tackle and get slaughtered. It only takes a moment of skill from an attacker or a misjudgement in the challenge to put you in real trouble.

"You can get booked so easily these days. But I defy anybody to say I've got a bad disciplinary record.

"My game is all about the desire to win. That's something every top player must have inside him." ■

bruce dyer
crystal palace

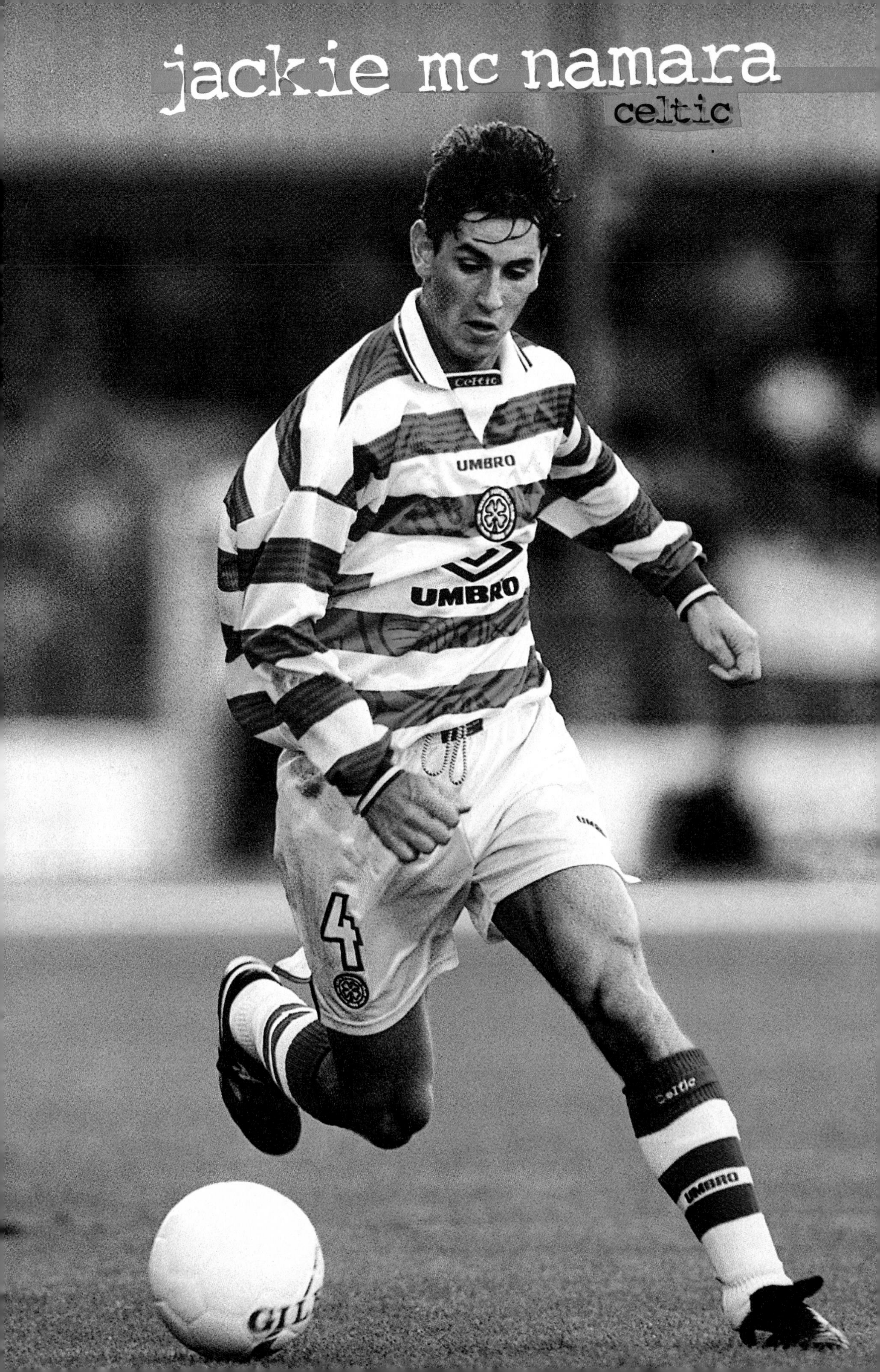
jackie mc namara
celtic
UMBRO
UMBRO

end of the road

THE Volcano is now dormant. The Tasmanian Devil has become an angel. Finally, Paolo Di Canio seems to have found peace at Sheffield Wednesday. Nicknamed "The Volcano" by former Wednesday manager, Ron Atkinson, because of his tempestuous nature, the Italian star has been the model of professionalism since his £3.5 million switch from Celtic two summers ago. He has even captained the side in the absence of regular skipper, Peter Atherton.

This was not what Wednesday fans were expecting.

A crowd-pleasing talent with showy white boots to match, Di Canio thrilled Celtic fans with his talent and then disappointed them with the manner of his departure. The pay dispute that preceded his arrival in England made him appear the typical money-grabbing foreigner.

Add in his infamous on-pitch histrionics, and little wonder many Wednesday fans had serious reservations about their record signing's staying power. They have since been proved very wrong.

The man who lifts his Wednesday shirt to reveal a Tasmanian Devil top has shown himself to be as much a part of Sheffield as a piece of steel cutlery.

He may no longer be challenging for European honours at Juventus or AC Milan but life at Sheffield Wednesday is as sweet as it has ever been.

Says Paolo, "I love it in

> **"I love it in Sheffield and would like to finish my career here."**

Sheffield and would like to finish my career here. The atmosphere is right for me.

"The people like me and that is important. I love it when they sing my name. When you have a situation like that, it makes you want to give them a bit extra on the pitch.

"I was made captain for a few games just eight months after joining the club. That made me so proud.

"Few foreign players have led sides in England. It is difficult because of language problems. But I was considered responsible enough very early on.

"I captained Celtic in my final few months there and led Juventus - one of the biggest sides in the world - in a tournament in Turin. Wearing the Wednesday armband equalled that.

"Some players just want to play for Arsenal, Manchester United or Liverpool because they are big clubs. Sometimes, though, it is better to be at a smaller club because there is a better feeling and a greater chance of playing every game.

"I've played for Juventus and AC Milan, yet I didn't play every game and that made me sad. That isn't the case in England and that is why I love playing for Sheffield Wednesday.

"I've won a Serie A title, UEFA Cup, European Cup and Scottish Player of the Year awards and I don't think I could handle not playing all the time.

"Most Italian players thinking of moving to England want to go to London clubs but I'm glad I'm in Yorkshire. London is a fantastic city but I wouldn't like to live there.

"Although I'm from Rome, my home in Italy is 40 minutes away from the city in Umbria. It is a lovely, quiet country area. I enjoy similar surroundings in Sheffield.

> **"London is a fantastic city but I wouldn't like to live there."**

"I like a good atmosphere for my family and that is not possible in a big city like London or Rome. They are incredible places but have incredible traffic problems.

"You can visit them on holiday for maybe a week but if you work there, it is terrible. I prefer the quiet life."

The tranquility in the Di Canio household is only broken when a certain cartoon character appears on the television.

He explains, "I watch a lot of cartoons with my daughter, Ludovica, and my favourite is the Tasmanian Devil. He is my hero.

"One day when we were out shopping, she noticed a T-shirt with the character on the front. She thought it was perfect for me and reckoned that if I wore it in the next game against Southampton, we would win.

"I forgot about it and wore a plain white shirt in the first half of the game. It wasn't until we were back in the changing rooms that I remembered what she had said and put it on. We went on to win the game 1-0.

"I've worn it ever since, even though we haven't won every game. It is my lucky charm."

He feels so at home in Sheffield that he even has visions of becoming a future Sheffield Wednesday manager.

Says Paolo, "I'm still young and want to continue playing for a

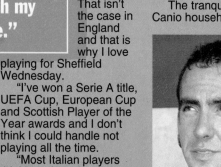

good while yet. However, with Attillio Lombardo having managed Crystal Palace last season and Gianluca Vialli doing well at Chelsea, I think management would be an incredible experience for me.

"I'm not a Capello, Lippi or Trappatoni, but I've played under them at Juventus and Milan and I've gained a lot of knowledge from them. I think I would do a good job.

"I've been in football for 15 years and travelled Europe to play the game. I understand football and know which tactics work and those that don't.

"Having good players isn't enough. To win anything you have to have good players who are also intelligent.

"My dream is still to play at Wembley in a Cup Final for Sheffield Wednesday. After that I would love the chance to manage the club.

"I reckon I could emulate Vialli. Moving from player to manager was a big advantage to him.

"The players got to know him and like him as a normal person before he moved up.

"It is important that players like their manager. If they don't, he won't get the best performance out of them." ■

Scotland and Blackburn Rovers striker Kevin Gallacher, a regular goalscorer for club and country, is one of the most naturally-gifted strikers in the Premiership. His six goals in the World Cup qualifying campaign ensured Scotland's appearance in the Finals last summer.

Previously with Dundee United and Coventry, Kevin has scored many memorable goals in his career. We asked him to name his favourite ten.

1
Dundee United 4, Celtic 2. Scottish Premier League, January 4th, 1986.
Celtic were my boyhood heroes and they were on the receiving end of my first goal in senior football. A low cross came in and I nipped in front of full back Danny McGrain to score at the near post.

2
Dundee United 1, Barcelona 0. UEFA Cup quarter final first leg, March 4th, 1987.
In the early stages I sent in a looping effort that sailed over Barca keeper Zubizarreta into the far corner of the net. After the game, I said on television that I had meant to shoot. Barcelona's coach Terry Venables said, "If the lad was honest enough he would say that he tried to cross the ball!" I have left people guessing ever since! We reached the final that season but lost to Gothenburg.

3
Celtic 2, Dundee United 1. Scottish Cup Final, May 14th, 1988.
It was our second consecutive Cup Final, and was to end in our second consecutive defeat. A Celtic goal-kick was headed back by United's Eamonn Bannon. I was in a race with Celtic captain Roy Aitken who was mindful that, after an earlier booking, he couldn't foul me or he would be sent off. I hit a volley with the outside of my left foot into the top corner. It took such an effort that I thought it was the 89th minute, but it was only the 49th.

4
Coventry City 5, Nottingham Forest 4. Rumbelows Cup, November 28th, 1990.
This was my first hat-trick in English football. Forest's Nigel Clough also scored a hat-trick that night, but I ended up with the ball because mine came first. Two of the goals were tap-ins but the third was a goal similar to the one I scored against Barcelona.

5
Estonia 0, Scotland 3. World Cup qualifier, May 19th, 1993.
My first international goal was a long time coming. It took me 16 internationals, although for most of those appearances I played wide and had few scoring chances. I had reached the stage where I thought I would never score for my country. Although it was just a tap-in, it was worth waiting for. I felt so proud.

6
Manchester United 1, Blackburn 1. Premiership, December 26th, 1993.
This was the best individual goal I have ever scored. I turned Gary Pallister, put it through Steve Bruce`s legs and when Peter Schmeichel raced from his goal to narrow the angle, I lifted it over him.

best

This was my return to action after being out for a year with a broken leg. I scored the goal that put us 2-0 ahead. However, I then suffered a hairline fracture and was carried from the pitch not to play again that season. We eventually won the match 2-1 and the three points proved invaluable as we won the Championship by just a single point. It meant that, although my appearance for the season lasted just an hour, I felt I made a contribution. I was given a Championship medal. It was the most crucial goal of my club career.

8 **Scotland 2, Austria 0. World Cup qualifier, April 2nd, 1997.**
I scored both our goals against the group winners in our World Cup qualifying campaign. The second goal is one I will never forget. It was a result we thoroughly deserved and it turned out to be the most important game in the campaign. I picked the ball up at the edge of the box and just let fly with a swerving volley that went in off the far post. The game was extra special because it was played at Celtic Park, where they had not held an international for over 60 years.

9 **Scotland 2, Latvia 0. World Cup qualifier, October 11th, 1997.**
We had to win this match to have a chance of automatic qualification to the Finals. My goal settled some early nerves when it arrived just before half-time. The goalkeeper spilled a shot from John Collins and I was on hand to head home. It was my sixth goal in five World Cup ties.

10 **Arsenal 1, Blackburn 3. Premiership, December 13th, 1997.**
This was the best shot I have ever scored with. I had never scored before with my left foot from outside the 18-yard box. The ball was flicked on by Chris Sutton. Tony Adams stood off me just enough for me to make up my mind to have a go. I volleyed over David Seaman and although he got his fingertips to it, the ball sailed into the net.

it's a funny old game

Referees are not often cheered off the field, but Ivan Robertson was when he was in charge of a 1968 League match between Barrow and Plymouth. He accidentally deflected the ball into the Barrow net to score the only goal of the game. To the Plymouth fans, he was a hero!

In 1986, a 52-year-old Argentinian cycled hundreds of miles to Mexico for the World Cup — only to find out that he could not afford the tickets! Then to make matters worse, someone stole his bike!

When organisers of the 1994 World Cup Finals in the United States advertised for security staff, applicants had to send in their thumb prints as well as their CV's. Fifty seven of them were then arrested for outstanding criminal charges!

Norwich City fans have claimed more than once to have seen a headless horseman approaching the Carrow Road ground from the River End and local ghost-busters have said that it is the spectre of Ned Ludmoore who was a local highwayman in the 17th century. Meanwhile, a ghostly group of Roman soldiers have allegedly been seen near York City's Bootham Crescent ground. Who says neither club has a ghost of a chance of getting into the Premiership?

Former Arsenal boss Don Howe must still be kicking himself for the day he turned down a Dutch teenager who was offered to him by Haarlem for just £80,000. Cautious Howe did not listen when he was told that the young man was one of the best prospects ever seen in Holland and as a result he missed out on signing Ruud Gullit!

"THAT'S A VERY CLOSE OFFSIDE CALL!"

"THAT WORLD CUP TRIP TO FRANCE HAS FAIR ALTERED YOUR HALF-TIME REFRESHMENT, SYD!"

Exeter assistant manager Noel Blake has the unusual middle names of LLOYD GEORGE, Mark Bright's middle name is ABRAHAM and there are some other strange ones about. What about Peter BOLESLAW Schmeichel, Craig LORNE Forrest or Pablo CESAR Wanchope? Favourite, though, has to be Emile WILLIAM IVANHOE Heskey.

"HEY THESE AIR SOLES REALLY WORK!"

"UNITED SEEM DETERMINED TO GET BIG TOM'S SIGNATURE!"

paul merson
middlesbrough

shoulder high!

Gary Brady on Spurs team-mate Jurgen Klinsmann

Dave Watson (Everton) on Dwight Yorke (Aston Villa)

Keith Gillespie (Newcastle Utd) on Alan Wright (Aston Villa)

mr versatility

t HERE was no one more surprised than Simon Grayson when he received a phone call from his former boss at Leicester City, Brian Little, offering him the opportunity to follow him to Aston Villa. The 28-year-old defender was in the throes of signing a new contract with City, but could not turn down the chance of linking up once again with the man he regards as his mentor.

But Grayson knew that the hard work was only just beginning. Although he had convinced Little that he had what it takes to be a success at Villa, he still had to convince himself, his new team-mates and the legions of Villa fans who would accept nothing but the best.

"When I joined Villa I expected it would be difficult to play every game. But I figured that even if I didn't play many games, Villa are still one of the top six clubs in the country," says Simon. "I have missed a few, but have been delighted to have featured so often.

"I know it was a bit of a gamble coming here. I was an established first-team player at Leicester and when I came to Villa I was initially just a squad player. But I have worked hard and got my rewards."

Grayson could have feared the worst when Little was replaced by John Gregory towards the end of last season. But the new man had as much faith in him as his predecessor.

"I feel that I always had the ability, but lacked a bit of confidence," Simon adds.

"I had been building up my confidence ever since I joined Leicester from Leeds for just £50,000 in 1991.

"Three play-off Finals and a Coca-Cola Cup Final with City did the trick, but the step up to Villa was a big boost for me. It finally brought it home to me that people appreciate what I am doing.

"The breakthrough came a couple of seasons ago with the Coca-Cola Cup win, but I feel I have gone up another level since coming to Villa.

"At last I feel I am fulfilling my potential. I have worked hard since I was a 16-year-old apprentice at Elland Road, though perhaps I have not had the headlines or the credit that I have deserved.

"I never gave up the hope that I could establish myself as a Premiership player. The only time in my career where I could say that I drifted was during the early days at Leeds. I did not play a first-team game for four seasons.

"But those days are long gone. I feel I have won over the Villa fans and, more importantly, gained the respect of my team-mates."

Grayson had to pinch himself last season when he looked over to the dug-out in some matches and spotted big-money buys Stan Collymore and Savo Milosevic unable to command a place in the side, while he had established himself as a regular.

But despite this, he is well down the queue when it comes to grabbing the headlines.

He goes on, "I don't get envious of others. I am not one who likes the idea of stardom, anyway. It is all right if you are playing well, but there is a downside if you are not.

> ## "I have been used mainly in midfield, although I have been used as a right-back and even a central defender on the odd occasion."

"The Villa fans were possibly a bit suspicious of me at first. I was not a big name and they may not have been convinced that I was good enough to pull on a Villa shirt but I like to think that I have now earned the respect of the Villa fans."

Grayson's biggest strength is his ability to adapt to any position. Under Little at Leicester, he played most of his games in midfield. But when Little left for Villa, Simon spent most of the following two seasons as a full-back.

When he linked up again with Little, he reverted back to midfield, where he has stayed.

Simon adds, "In the last two seasons at Leicester I played at full-back on both flanks.

"But since I joined Villa I have been used mainly in midfield, although I have been used as a right-back and even a central defender on the odd occasion.

"It means that I have a few strings to my bow and that could help me in my bid to hold down a regular place in the Villa side." ■

for better or verse!

WHAT do Marks and Spencer, London Zoo and Barnsley Football Club have in common? Answer: they all have a resident poet. Barnsley poet Ian McMillan puts into rhyme the highs and lows of supporting his local team.

Ian's writings appeal to fans because he IS a fan. He writes from the heart and, as he explains, that is why there will always be a place for poetry in football.

"Although they might not appear to have anything in common, football and poetry share a strong bond," says Ian. "Poetry is about passion, and, of course, so is football.

"The first football poem I wrote was back in 1974. Barnsley had played an away match at Stockport and it was a boring game. On the way back home, while driving over the moors, my uncle Donald told me that he would never go to another match. It was that bad. I then wrote 'The Away Match'."

Ian explains that his wish is to help spread the message that poetry is an enjoyable and light-hearted way of expressing one's thoughts and feelings about football.

"A couple of years ago, I was talking about this to a friend and he urged me to phone Barnsley Football Cub and offer my services as the club poet.

"I am surprised by the amount of attention I have received. I was going to send out a Press release, but I didn't have to. The local Press contacted me and it snowballed from there.

"I have written poems for national newspapers and even appeared on foreign television. A woman reporter from NBC television in America phoned me and asked, 'Can I come and interview you the next time Barnsley play at home?' How many other clubs can say they had American television turning up at their ground?

"Word certainly gets around. A journalist interviewed me and the article appeared in a German magazine. A German television crew saw it and came to speak to me. Then a Dutch reporter contacted me.

"The British Council in Mexico asked me if I would go over and recite some of my poetry. Apparently, I am regarded as an example of British culture there.

"I spent two weeks in Mexico doing some gigs and reciting to local students. I performed some of my football poems.

"It was great that I could cross the cultural divide between Barnsley and Mexico. I was also chuffed that the Mexicans had heard of Barnsley's exploits in the Premiership. Mind you, by the end of my stay I was trying to hide my loyalties. In that week we had lost 5-0 at Arsenal and 2-0 at home to Leicester!"

One of the Barnsley Poet's most celebrated works is called 'Ceefax.' It tells of a fan's obsession with watching the latest football scores on teletext.

"Ceefax just wrote itself," adds Ian. "My wife always wonders why I should watch a screen that hardly ever changes. She says I'm addicted to ceefax. That was one of the poems I recited in Mexico. Surprisingly, they seemed to understand it.

"Ironically, the match that inspired the poem did not even involve Barnsley. It was between Wolves and Grimsby in the season we won promotion from the First Division. Wolves had to win to keep the pressure on us. They went one up, but Grimsby equalised."

Ian wrote many of his poems last season as Barnsley enjoyed their first-ever season in the Premiership.

His writings were in great demand as the media sought a voice that captured the joys and anxieties of a small-town club struggling to survive among the country's elite.

Ian goes on, "One of the proudest days of my poetry career was when the Barnsley fans sang one of my poems at Pride Park, the home of Derby County.

"Our goalkeeper, Lars Leese, had just made a great save, and I heard our fans call out, 'Lars Leese, tall as trees that grow in Wombwell Wood.' I never thought I would pen a poem that would be sang in a ground.

"I wrote a poem to mark our visit to Anfield last season. It proved lucky because we beat Liverpool 1-0.

"Poetry is all about expressing oneself. Barnsley men are normally quite taciturn, but when it comes to football, it's a different story. On Saturdays there are more people at Oakwell than anywhere else in Barnsley. It is from sitting beside these fans that I get my inspirations." ∎

TOPICAL TIMES FOOTBALL BOOK

When I go to a match
make no mistake
I know exactly
what to take

Got my flask
and my sweets
got my rattle and my flag

and so much more
in my Barnsley bag!

And at half-time
when I drink my coffee
I know just what to do:
I open up my Topical Times
Football Book
and read a page or two...

(or three or four...)

(Specially written for the Topical Times)

CEEFAXANORAX

I'm a mad
sat in front of the ceefax
sad sack anorak
That's me!

I'm a sad
staring at the motionless ceefax
stone mad
anorak
That's me!

Come on you numbers change
Come on you Barnsley score
Come on you letters rearrange
Come on let's have one more!

I'm a daft
squatting before the ceefax
all adrift
Anorak
That's me
I'm adrift
floating before the ceefax
half daft
Anorak
that's me!

Come on you Ceefax watchers!
Come on you number crunchers
Come on you slumped on the settee
after too many liquid lunches!

We're all mad
Worshipping the ceefax
Half-daft
so sad
adrift
waiting for the score to change
Ceefaxanorax Ceefaxanorax
Ceefaxanorax

commercial break

But football is the number one priority for Spurs' DAVID GINOLA

f RENCH superstar David Ginola punctured some myths with his form for Tottenham Hotspur last season. When Ginola joined Spurs from Newcastle after a disappointing year on Tyneside, his critics claimed the flamboyant winger was only interested in joining the club so that he could enjoy the London night-club scene.

They said he would be more intent on promoting his modelling ambitions than his football career; that he would be a luxury player whom struggling Spurs would not be able to afford.

Spurs struggled all right. But David Ginola was outstanding all season, revealing unsuspected strength of character and determination, to help avoid the relegation threat. Ginola certainly accepted offers to do television commercials for cars and hair shampoo. But he was determined to avoid any adverse effect on his football.

"Football has always come first for me," says Ginola. "Football is definitely my priority. I am a professional. I do my job as well as I possibly can. Outside activities will never be allowed to interfere.

"I do the publicity jobs because I enjoy the work, and it pays well. But I will only accept offers if I have plenty of time to rest. My biggest pleasure comes on the football pitch. From a good shot, a piece of skill, or even just working up a good sweat in training.

"Fashion shoots are okay. I have nothing against them. But I would much prefer to see a picture of myself in a football paper, than in a fashion magazine.

"It gets on my nerves when people suggest my outside activities affect my football. That has never been true. The publicity work could all stop tomorrow, and I wouldn't be bothered.

"My life is well organised. It is as regular as an office worker's. My job comes first. Naturally I like to go out. After only two hours' training every day, you can get bored just staying at home.

"Instead of pacing about at home, I open my eyes to the world around me.

"It is a fact that I enjoy my football more now than I ever did. As I get nearer to the end of my career, I am more determined than ever to put everything into it. I tell myself that every match has to be fantastic. Football is the most important thing for me.

"My life is in place. I enjoy living in London. It is a different world, and I have met some nice people.

"The only negative thing about last season was that we weren't getting results."

> **"I would much prefer to see a picture of myself in a football paper, than in a fashion magazine."**

Ginola signed a four-year contract at Spurs last year, after failing to establish a rapport with new manager Kenny Dalglish at Newcastle.

"I had eighteen great months with Kevin Keegan at Newcastle, but after he left it became difficult," admits David.

"It's important for me to have a good relationship with the people I work with. That just didn't happen in the last six months at St. James' Park.

"I had to break off that relationship, and start again somewhere else. Spurs were the only club prepared to pay £2m for a thirty- year- old player.

"I didn't have much choice, but I have no regrets at all. Tottenham is a very big club, with great potential. It is a club that seems to have been asleep for a few years. I want to do everything to help turn things round.

"Spurs were always one of the

clubs I liked to watch on television as a youngster. I remember the famous white shirts. I can remember when they were one of the biggest clubs in Europe. I want to help them regain that position.

"People in France wonder why I want to play in England. They say it doesn't suit my game.

"But they play attacking football in the Premier League. I just love playing with the ball at my feet.

"I have been in England for three years, and I know it is one of the best leagues in the world. The games are exciting, the fans are passionate, and I enjoy being on the pitch.

"I didn't come to have an easy time. I'm not in semi-retirement. I want to win things in England. I have never worked so hard at the game.

"I believe I am a better player now. More complete. At Spurs I am not restricted to the left wing, and I enjoy being more involved in the game.

"But nothing makes me happier than winning matches. That's the best thing in football. I hope I will be very happy this season." ■

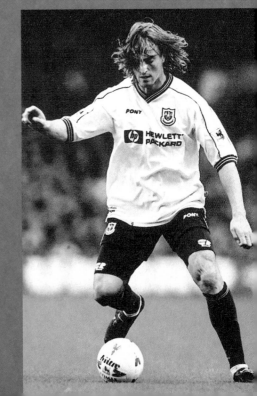

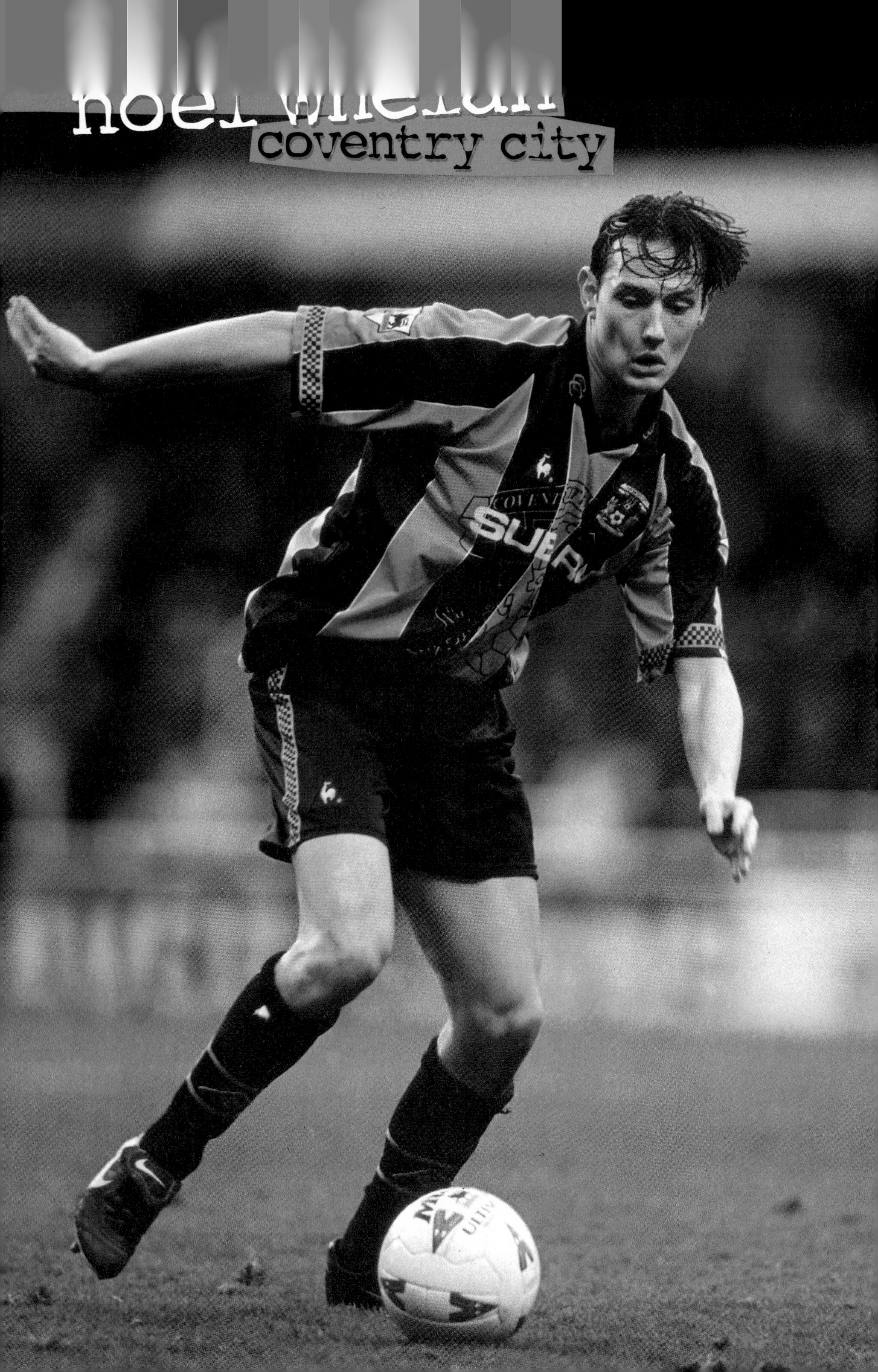
coventry city

sol campbell

spurs

star in the making

Famous? Not yet — but Leeds United LUCAS RADEBE

s working on it!

SOUTH AFRICAN Lucas Radebe is one of the least-known foreigners in the Premiership, but he can count on a bigger following than Dennis Bergkamp, Gianfranco Zola and Peter Schmeichel put together!

The Leeds United defender retains a low profile in England despite becoming one of the most consistent performers in the top flight. However, in his native South Africa, Radebe is idolised by millions.

Lucas would not mind acquiring the same star status in Leeds that he enjoys in South Africa, but he will settle for a regular game in the United first team

That is because he believes he is indebted to Leeds and every good performance goes towards a repayment of that debt.

Says Lucas, "My first couple of years at Leeds were very disappointing. A serious knee injury made it very hard for me to settle at the club and I was always wanting to go back home to see my family.

"I was a stranger in England and I wasn't able to do the job I was brought here to do, so I was homesick for virtually a whole season.

"I never felt like packing my bags and going home, though. I missed South Africa but I knew I had to stay at Leeds and prove myself.

"My injury was a cruciate ligament problem. When I looked at it after it had happened, it was very bad and I didn't think that I would play top-flight football again.

"I was very frightened about my future. When the doctor told me that I would have to have surgery, it took my breath away and I thought that my dream was over.

"The people at Leeds told me that I could recover and as soon as I heard that I told myself that I would play again and show everybody what I could do.

"I came to the club with my fellow South African, Phil Masinga, and he made a great start at Leeds and scored important goals. He became a crowd favourite, but I was forgotten about.

"We were both determined to succed, though, because we knew that we were ambassadors for our country. We didn't want to fail because we wanted to help other South Africans earn a move to England.

"Unfortunately, Howard Wilkinson, who was the manager at the time, didn't have much confidence in us. Phil lost his work permit, but I was given another one because of my injury. That was when my luck began to change.

"The following season, I went away with South Africa to play in the African Nations Cup. I hadn't played all season and only went to build up my fitness.

"However, I played in all our games and we won the tournament. I returned to Leeds fully fit and never looked back. Injuries forced the manager to put me in the team

> **"I enjoy the role because it helps me appear on Match of the Day!"**

and I kept my place."

It was not until George Graham replaced Howard Wilkinson as Leeds manager in 1996 that Lucas began to feel like a fully-fledged member of the first team.

Lucas goes on, "I was worried when George Graham took over because I knew nothing about him and he probably didn't know much about me. He put me in the team as a man-marker, though, and put me on the opposition's best player.

"I enjoy the role because it helps me appear on Match of the Day! Normally, nobody would notice me, but when I am marking Steve McManaman, Gianfranco Zola or Dennis Bergkamp, everybody can see me.

"If I play well, people will remark on it. That's how players like me are noticed. I love the role and look forward to marking the best players.

"I always give my best, though, because I feel that I owe the club a lot. I didn't earn my wages when I came here because of my injury, so every game I play is an opportunity to repay them."

Nobody in South Africa would claim that Radebe is in debt to his home country. As part of the team that qualified for the 1998 World Cup finals, Lucas became an instant hero and, as team captain, he was soon a figure that mixed in the highest circles.

Lucas reveals, "I was handed the captaincy before our final two qualifying games. It was a nervous time for the whole country, but we beat Congo in our final game and qualified.

"It was unreal to think about being in the World Cup. I had watched the 1994 tournament and never believed I would ever play in the finals.

"There was a huge party after we qualified, but I had to return to Leeds. Before we played Congo, I had dinner with President Mandela because I was the captain and he promised to declare a national holiday on the Monday if we went through. That was great, but I wasn't around to enjoy it.

"I would have had to hide under my baseball cap if I had stayed. People can recognise me without it and they shout over to me and talk to me. I don't mind it all. I love being famous and it would be nice to become so popular in Leeds.

"When I was young, I used to think that footballers were out of reach of normal people. Now I know that isn't true and if I am a superstar to a young boy, I think that is fantastic". ■

Celebrating World Cup qualification.

Frank Leboeuf (Chelsea) v. Kevin Gallacher (Blackburn Rovers)

Henning Berg (Man.Utd) v. Dennis Bergkamp (Arsenal)

double

Andreas Andersson (Newcastle United) v. Slaven Bilic (Everton)

Emile Heskey (Leicester City) v. Gary Mabbutt (Spurs)

action!

A split-frame look at the Premiership!

Darren Huckerby (Coventry City) v. Lee Carsley (Derby County)

Can it get any better for

T'S A long way from the humble surroundings of Motherwell's Fir Park to the splendour of the Olympic Stadium in Munich and the glory of European Cup triumph.

But for Celtic midfielder Paul Lambert, Borussia Dortmund's unforgettable against- the-odds triumph over Juventus in the 1997 European Cup Final was only the START of the best 12 months of his football career.

Indeed, you could easily be forgiven for thinking the cultured midfielder is a man with the Midas touch!

Within a year of hoisting Europe's premier club trophy aloft as part of the Dortmund side who brought the European Cup to the Ruhr for the first time, Lambert was celebrating back in his homeland after helping Celtic end Rangers' decade-long domination of the Premier League title.

Throw in the small matter of a starring role for Craig Brown's World Cup side in France '98 and it's fair to say Paul had a pretty remarkable year!

And, as he reveals, his perfect

beat that!

year was all thanks to current RANGERS manager Dick Advocaat!

"After I left Motherwell, I was offered a trial at PSV Eindhoven, who were then managed by Dick Advocaat, " says Paul.

"I played twice for PSV on a trial basis, and even managed to score in both games, which is pretty unusual for me!

"However, Advocaat told me that I wasn't quite what he was looking for, and that he was looking for a winger while I always play in the middle. So in the end I went to Dortmund—and that didn't work out too badly for me!

"When I arrived there, I was in awe of guys like Andy Moeller and

Matthias Sammer, but they helped me settle in straight away. That was a huge help, especially since my family hadn't found it all that easy to settle in Germany.

"I was a little surprised to get a starting place so quickly and I knew I had to perform to the very best of my abilities in each and every game

if I was to retain a first-team place.

"Having played for smaller clubs, St Mirren and Motherwell, in Scotland, it was incredible to be playing in front of 50,000, in a team of world class players, week in, week out."

Dortmund kept their best form that season for the Champions'

Celtic's PAUL LAMBERT?

League and a sparkling run — including home and away victories over Manchester United — saw them reach the final against the mighty Juventus, ironically at the home of Dortmund's great rivals, Bayern Munich.

"I never usually get nervous before big games," laughs the cultured midfielder, "but, on that occasion, I did get a slight twinge walking out alongside Alessandro Del Piero and company!

"Once the game started, though, I was okay and I even managed to get forward and cross for Karl-Heinz Riedle to open the scoring after half an hour.

"That was probably the best team performance we produced during my spell at Dortmund and we fully deserved to run out 3-1 winners.

"Lifting the European Cup was an incredible feeling, but the reception I was given by the Dortmund fans after my final game was even more emotional for me.

"I had a wonderful time in Germany and made a lot of great friends but I also improved 100% as a footballer.

"The coaching I had under Ottmar Hitzfeld was incredible and I owe a lot of my success to his influence and to playing and learning alongside exceptional talents like Moeller, Sammer and Riedle."

His Bundesliga experience transformed Lambert from a playmaker into one of the best defensive midfield players in

Europe with the Champions' League medal to prove it.

Celtic, after splashing out £2-million to bring the 28-year-old back to Scotland, were set to reap the benefit as Wim Jansen's side battled to wrest the Premier Division crown from Old Firm rivals Rangers for the first time in a decade.

"I decided to come back home partly because my family never totally settled in Germany," reveals Paul, "but the challenge of trying to end Rangers' domination of Scottish football also appealed."

But, when Lambert arrived, that prospect looked an unrealistic one, with Celtic trailing their ancient rivals in the table after a shaky start to the Wim Jansen era. Then came the New Year's Day encounter between the Glasgow giants and it was that game that confirmed the Scotland star's hero status in the eyes of the Celtic fans.

"We knew going into that game that if we could take all three points we'd be in with a great chance of overhauling Rangers.

"The omens weren't good, though. Celtic hadn't beaten Rangers in ten years in the New Year fixture and Rangers had held the upper hand in the previous two League matches that season.

"We were all over them early on but Andy Goram was, as usual, producing some miraculous saves to keep us out.

"As the game wore on, I think a

few of the players must have thought 'Here we go again!'

"But Craig Burley produced a great finish to finally break the deadlock. Then, with a couple of minutes left, I let fly from about 25 yards and the ball just seemed to fly into the top corner. It was probably the best shot I've struck in my career and certainly my favourite goal.

"After that result, I think everyone in the squad realised it was going to be our season, if we kept displaying the same determination.

"We kept our nerve, even though we needed a last-day victory over St Johnstone, to pip Rangers to the title.

"Winning the Premier League title was as important to me as the European Cup because of what it meant to everyone connected with the club to stop Rangers making it ten-in-a-row.

"From a personal point of view, it was great to win the League in my own country, with all my family watching."

Sadly for Paul, Celtic's title celebrations were almost immediately cut short by the bombshell news that enigmatic Dutch coach Wim Jansen was quitting the club.

"That was a real blow to me because, after Ottmar Hitzfeld, Wim was the coach I learned most from. All the players were gutted that he quit and, at the time, I even questioned my own future at the club."

But, that had to be put aside for the very good reason that a meeting with the World Champions beckoned in France!

"I suppose, for my first ever game in the World Cup Finals, to play against holders Brazil in the opening match wasn't too bad!" laughs Paul.

"But, given the way things had gone for me in the previous 12 months, I guess I shouldn't have been surprised at all!" ■

> **"Lifting the European Cup was an incredible feeling, but the reception I was given by the Dortmund fans after my final game was even more emotional for me."**

shay given
newcastle united

the 90-minute man!

Football means total involvement for Leicester City's ROB SAVAGE

dURING the first few months of his career with Leicester City, Rob Savage took great delight in claiming more female fans than the rest of the City players.

With his long hair and pop-star looks, the 24-year-old midfielder was an obvious target for the teenage girls among the autograph hunters.

Naturally, he was immediately dubbed 'Glamour Boy' by mocking team-mates. Being one of the livelier members of the Filbert Street dressing room himself, Rob was happy to join in the fun.

One year on, Savage's group of admirers has grown, and for reasons which delight him even more. During that time, his ability on the football pitch has been widely recognised and he has become a well-established member of the Leicester first team.

This means that Savage is well ahead of the schedule which he set for himself when he signed for the club during the summer of 1997.

On leaving his previous club, Crewe Alexandra, Rob believed it would take most of his first season to adjust to the demands of Premiership football. But he made an early impact and was soon a regular member of manager Martin O'Neill's line-up, although he had to work hard to keep his place.

Says Rob, "I have had to become fitter than I have ever been in my life in order to meet the demands posed by life at Premiership level. As the midfield man who does a lot of the fetching and carrying, I have to cover most of the pitch.

"I like to be involved all the time, buzzing around the play at both ends of the field. I have great stamina, which allows me to get forward whenever we attack and back to help out in defence whenever we are under threat."

In making his mark, Savage has fulfilled a prophecy once made by Manchester United manager Alex Ferguson. But he admits that he first had to show his current boss just how hard he was prepared to work.

"I came up through the youth ranks at Old Trafford and played in the same team as David Beckham, Nicky Butt, Paul Scholes and the Neville brothers Gary and Phil," Rob recalls. "The club gave me a professional contract after we won the FA Youth Cup.

"In all, I had three years with them just before they all broke through to the first team.

"But during my final year at Old Trafford, I had a double hernia which kept me out of action for six months. Once I was fit, the manager told me he was letting me go. It was the worst day of my life. I was devastated.

"But Alex left me with a bit of hope when he told me that I would play in the Premiership one day. I just don't think he expected I would achieve it so quickly.

"But I have worked hard to reach that status, and that effort fits in very well with Leicester City, who are a hard-working side and all battle for one another.

"I think I had to convince Martin O'Neill of that, because my appearance may have suggested I was a bit different. I recognised that I probably had the look of a flashy player, and that is definitely not Martin O'Neill's style. In fact, I have always been a committed player, and worked very hard to show him that.

"I think he soon realised how much effort I was prepared to put in, and I'm glad that was rewarded with a regular place." ■

made in

Monaco!

MART POOM'S Derby County career had an unusual start!

ERBY COUNTY goalkeeper Mart Poom is probably the only footballer in the world that measures his popularity by the strength of the 'booing' he receives whenever he touches the ball!

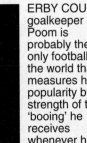

He is also a rarity among footballers in that he finished third in a sportsman of the year contest behind a decathlete and a fencer and was flattered to be voted into such a high position.

The Estonian number one earned rave reviews last year in his first full season in the Premiership. The fact that he spent most of his spare time at the club training ground probably explains why he did so well for the Pride Park outfit.

Poom admits he is a workaholic in search of perfection. He is keen to surpass Peter Schmeichel as the top goalkeeper in the Premiership, but he is also desperate to make the most of his second chance in England after being forced to leave previous club, Portsmouth, because of work permit regulations.

Mart explains, "I spent two years at Portsmouth but had a bad knee injury, only played four League games and ended up losing my work permit.

"I had to play in at least three-quarters of Portsmouth's competitive fixtures, but I was miles away from that figure. My permit was revoked and I had to go back to Estonia and start again.

"While I was back home I had a couple of injuries. I broke my nose and then developed a hernia problem, so I didn't expect to earn another move abroad quickly.

"I spent three months in Cyprus training with the national team, however. Our winter in Estonia was too bad for us to train at home, so we had to base ourselves in Cyprus to prepare for a game against Scotland in Monaco, back in February 1997.

"That was the game that put me back on the map. It was a re-arranged game because the initial match in Estonia was abandoned after we failed to turn up on time.

"We held Scotland to a 0-0 draw and I had a good game and caught the eye of Derby manager, Jim Smith.

> "Jim was looking for a new goalkeeper and he remembered me from his time as Portsmouth boss. He signed me for Derby after that Scotland game."

"Jim was looking for a new goalkeeper and he remembered me from his time as Portsmouth boss. He signed me for Derby after that Scotland game.

"As soon as I arrived at Derby, I was handed my debut against Manchester United at Old Trafford. I had supported them as a boy and was also a big fan of Peter Schmeichel, so to make my debut there and win 3-2 was amazing.

"I have always believed that Schmeichel, David Seaman and Nigel Martyn are among the best goalkeepers in Europe, if not the world.

"That is my target and why I work so hard. I set high standards for myself and want to improve all the time. That is why I spend my afternoons at the training ground.

"I have always trained hard and I am used to two sessions a day. If we don't have a midweek game, I spend two or three afternoons with my coach, Eric Stevens.

"We do special goalkeeper work or weight-training and most times I stay on until about half past four. I don't think that is late, but most of my team-mates have gone home about three hours earlier.

"I believe that I can move into that top bracket alongside Schmeichel, Seaman and Martyn. Last year was only my first season in the Premiership but I learned a lot and I am getting better all the time.

"The supporters at Derby appreciate me and that helps. I must admit, however, that I was a bit worried about them when I first came to the club.

"Every time I made a good save or took a goal-kick they seemed to be booing me. I was very confused because they didn't look like they were

booing. There was no anger on their faces.

"It turned out that they were chanting my name, or at least attempting to. Unfortunately, I thought they were booing me because they were saying 'Poom.' My name is pronounced 'Porm,' so it took me a while to realise what they were doing!"

Poom has become a cult figure in Derby, but he is also making an impression back in Estonia, a country not noted for its passion for football.

Mart adds, "When I came third in the national awards for sportsmen it was a real achievement to finish behind a decathlete and a fencer. Estonians tend to prefer individual sportsmen instead of those involved in team sports. Finishing third was remarkable for a footballer and I was delighted.

"You can see how football is catching on back home. When I go back to my home in Tallinn, I now see young boys playing football in the streets. That is something new.

"Interest in football is growing and if that has anything to do with my performances for Derby, I couldn't be happier." ∎

Alan Shearer, of Newcastle United and England, whose goal-scoring exploits have made him one of the most feared strikers in the world. Twenty-five yard rockets, bullet headers or two-foot tap-ins...they are all in the repertoire of...

The Goal King

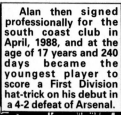

Alan Shearer was born in Newcastle on the 13th of August, 1970. He began his football career with Wallsend Boys' Club which he joined when he was 10. This club has turned out over thirty professional footballers including Steve Bruce and Peter Beardsley.

As a thirteen-year-old schoolboy, Alan spent a week on trial with Newcastle United, but he failed to impress. Nevertheless, talent scout Jack Hixon snapped him up for Southampton.

Alan then signed professionally for the south coast club in April, 1988, and at the age of 17 years and 240 days became the youngest player to score a First Division hat-trick on his debut in a 4-2 defeat of Arsenal.

Alan spent eight years at the Dell before moving to Blackburn Rovers for the record fee of £3.3m. He scored twice on his debut in a 3-3 draw with Crystal Palace.

By now Alan had achieved England recognition, scoring 13 goals in 11 appearances for the Under-21 team. He made his full England debut against France in February, 1992, scoring England's second goal in a 2-0 win.

In season 1994-95 his 34 Premiership goals helped Blackburn to their first Championship for 81 years. On top of this, he was voted PFA Player of the Year.

Although scoring regularly for his club, Alan went through 13 international games without an England goal. All this changed, however, in Euro '96 when he became the tournament's top scorer with five goals, including one in the semi-final against Germany.

Alan was now England captain and smashed the world transfer record when Newcastle United manager Kevin Keegan lured him back to Tyneside for £15m. He celebrated his home debut in customary style — by scoring from a 20-yard free-kick.

Alan was hit with a series of injuries which forced him to miss the opening months of season 1997-98 plus some vital World Cup qualifiers with England. But a fit Alan Shearer will always score goals, and he played a captain's role in Newcastle's run to the FA Cup Final, and in England's World Cup campaign in France last summer.

Shearer's World Cup dream last summer ended in bitter disappointment, scoring only two goals before England's second round penalty shoot-out defeat by Argentina. However, barring injury, Alan looks certain to continue to be a vital member of Glenn Hoddle's squad as one of England's most potent goal threats.

for ever

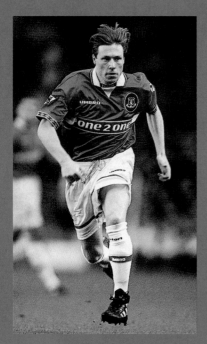

ICK BARMBY could quite easily have joined the procession of big-name players who left Everton last season.

Even though the Goodison Park club were constantly battling against relegation to the First Division, manager Howard Kendall decided that the only way to raise funds for new players was to sell his best performers.

Top international players like Gary Speed and Andy Hinchcliffe left the club, as did former internationalists David Unsworth, Earl Barrett and Neville Southall.

Big names were replaced by low-profile signings, but Barmby, the club record buy at £5.75 million, remained at the club. Everton could have cashed in on the England star, especially as he was struggling to force his way into Kendall's plans.

However, the former Spurs and Middlesbrough forward was determined to stay on Merseyside and prove his worth to his new manager.

Barmby knew that people were waiting for him to kick up a fuss. He was languishing in the reserves less than a year after his record transfer from Middlesbrough and his England career seemed like a distant memory. Nick refused to buckle. Instead, he worked away in the reserves and eventually won Kendall over.

Says Nick, "The start of last season was difficult for me. The arrival of Howard Kendall was a reminder that you can't take anything for granted in football and I found myself out of the team.

"I wasn't the only one. The manager took a long, hard look at his squad and he tried other players. I was left on the sidelines for a while and it took me a long time to force my way into his plans.

"Until late November, I was lucky to get a place on the bench. That was hard to take and I did wonder whether the boss fancied me as a player. My only route back was through the reserves and doing well in training.

"As the record signing at the club, I know that a lot of people were just waiting for me to come out and say that I wanted to leave.

"I suppose it would have been a good story for the newspapers, but I never once said that I wanted a transfer. I really like being at Everton.

"I didn't enjoy playing in the reserves, but in hindsight it did me

> "I am determined to be at the club when the good times return. I am just hoping that they aren't too far away."

good. Nobody has a divine right to play every week, but there are times when things don't go well and you have to prove a point.

"The fact that I didn't moan about things may have had a positive impression on the manager. Perhaps he saw me in a different light as a result.

"His opinion of me matters. Outside the game, people have an impression of me, but they don't know me. I don't care what they think, but it is important to earn the respect of the people you work with.

"I know that I disappointed a few people by keeping quiet and working away, but as things stand now, I feel as though my attitude has paid off.

"After returning to the team, things went well for me. I was even handed the captaincy for three games when regular skipper, Duncan Ferguson, was suspended. That was a massive honour and it made everything worthwhile.

"After being frozen out at the start of the season, it was a real boost to receive the armband. At 24, I am one of the older heads in this team and I know that some of the youngsters perhaps look up to me. That doesn't worry me.

"I know what it can be like to be a youngster in a struggling team and you do need the help of the older lads at times. We had some difficult times last season and I'm sure the young lads found it tough.

"The club was struggling at the wrong end of the table, but the likes of Michael Ball, John Oster and

ton!

with the Toffees!

Gavin McCann came in and handled the situation remarkably well.

"In one game last year, I was the third oldest player in the team. I'm only 24, so that sums up how many youngsters had come in last season."

That situation was a far cry from Barmby's early days at Goodison. On arriving from Middlesbrough in November 1996, Nick found himself in a team capable of challenging for the Championship.

He goes on, "Joe Royle was in charge when I came to Everton and I feel he was desperately unlucky in his final few weeks at the club.

"The early signs when I arrived here were very positive. I remember scoring in a 1-0 win at Derby which took us to fifth in the table. People were talking about us being dark horses for the title.

"It's not hard to see why. We had players like Andrei Kanchelskis, Gary Speed, Duncan Ferguson and Andy Hinchcliffe all playing at the top of their form.

"Unfortunately, Andy and Joe Parkinson sustained bad injuries which ended their season at an early stage. We never recovered and a few months later, Joe Royle lost his job. It was purely down to those injuries.

"Everton have struggled ever since, but I am determined to be at the club when the good times return. I am just hoping that they aren't too far away."

With the rebuilding of Everton now firmly under way, Nick is hoping his return to favour at Goodison Park will sustain his revitalised international fortunes.

Nick goes on, "When I was playing in the reserves last season, England coach Glenn Hoddle kept in touch with me and basically let me know that I was still in his plans.

"He told me that I couldn't be considered for England while I was playing reserve-team football, though. I knew that all along, but the fact that he had the decency to tell me in person meant a lot.

"It was good to know that I hadn't been forgotten. Glenn didn't have to phone me, but it's a mark of the man that he did.

"Still, it was a surprise when I was called into the 'B' squads during the World Cup build-up. It was good to be back in the fold. If things continue to go well for me at Everton, I can give myself a chance of making the next step up into the full squad." ■

jorg albertz
rangers

alessandro del piero
juventus

What an end to the season for Hearts' DAVID WEIR!

THERE might never be another year like it, but Hearts' David Weir will be able to live off the happy memories of the past 12 months for the rest of his life! Not only did Hearts have one of their best-ever seasons but David ended the season with a cup-winner's medal — and a trip to France on World Cup business with Scotland!

Says David, "Season 1997-98 began like any other — in fact, it got off to a worse start than usual — but, by the start of June 98, my football career had gone into orbit.

"A year earlier, Hearts had gone through their customary pre-season work-out at Musselburgh, and boss Jim Jefferies had added only two new first-teamers in Frenchman Stephane Adam and Thomas Flogel from Austria.

"That pair were to make their mark at Tynecastle, but everyone at the club pulled together week in, week out, and now we can say with some conviction that we are the third biggest club in the land."

Yet in what was to become a season to change the Jam Tarts' history books, it all started badly. While their Edinburgh arch-rivals, Hibs, defeated Celtic, who had splashed out millions on new big names,

> ## "By the start of June 98, my football career had gone into orbit."

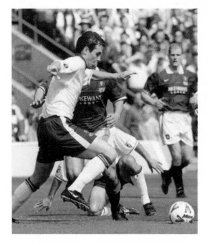

Hearts lost to Rangers at Ibrox — and in the next few weeks some critics predicted a title challenge from Hibs, and a relegation battle for Hearts. "However," continues David, "by September, Jim had us operating the way he wanted, and a superb victory over Kilmarnock — when I scored with a header from a Steve Fulton corner — saw us on top of the Premier Division.

"Hearts have been there before, of course, for a week or two while the seasons are just getting going, but there was a real belief that we could stay at the top this time. That says a lot about the self-respect Jim and his assistant, Billy Brown, had instilled in us.

"Ever since his days at Falkirk, the gaffer has always been a no-nonsense type of coach, and he rarely looks at what our main rivals are doing. Everything is 'What can WE do to change this?' and it's all about team spirit at his clubs.

"As far as we were concerned, Rangers and Celtic could fill their squads with household names from all over Europe and beyond — and they could take the majority of points when we played them — but, so long as we took care of our fixtures with the other seven sides, we'd be in with a chance."

Manager Jefferies knew that Hearts could not compete with the Old Firm financially but installed in his side a strong team spirit and made sure the club had a good youth policy.

Such a policy saw the emergence of young stars like Young Scottish Player of the Year Gary Naysmith and Paul Ritchie.

Sadly, Hearts' title challenge faltered in the latter part of the season, but the Tynecastle side were determined to end the season on a high note with a victory over Rangers in the Scottish Cup Final.

Says David, "Few outside Tynecastle believed we could win. Hearts hadn't lifted the Cup for 42 years, while Rangers had won at least one trophy each season for the past 12 years. In fact, we'd only reached four Scottish Cup

final glo

Finals since 1956, and lost the lot!

"Rangers were used to success, but this was their last chance to win something before Walter Smith moved aside and his team broke up. Jim, though, was determined that, as usual, we should just concentrate on how much WE wanted victory.

"On the day, we made the perfect start with a first-minute penalty and Steve Fulton ran the midfield while Gilles Rousset had

TENNENT'S LAGER   TENNENT'S LAGER

TENNENTS SCOTTISH CUP WINNERS 1997/98

a great game in goal. When our other Frenchman, Stephane Adam, scored a second, the shock was on.

"The last 10 minutes, though, after Ally McCoist pulled a goal back, were the first time I saw Jim Jefferies really feeling the pressure all season.

"But we held on to beat that 'nearly men' tag, and now I believe Jim can lead us to a lot more success in the future." ∎

ry!

a tale of the
unexpec
starring ROLAND NILSSON

mOST footballers dread the thought of retirement. After years of concentrating mind, body and soul on the game, coming to terms with life without football can be hard to accept.

Coventry City's Roland Nilsson, though, has thought of little else for the last few years. He has no fears about it. His only concern is when to do it!

By joining the Sky Blues two summers ago, the former Sheffield Wednesday defender put back one retirement date. Now he is enjoying his football so much at Highfield Road that he hopes to ruin another plan to hang up his boots!

Says Roland, "When I decided to leave Wednesday and return to Sweden in 1994, I honestly thought that was it. I took my bow in front of the fans and I thought I was walking out on English football for good.

"My plan was to play for a couple of seasons back home and then retire from the game completely. I was convinced that was how it would turn out.

"I played for Helsingborgs and had a good time. They are one of the top sides in the country. We played European football in both years I was there and I was still in the Swedish national side.

"It wasn't until Coventry made an offer to the club that I even considered carrying on. It was completely out of the blue.

"It wasn't something I was hoping for and I didn't send out any signals that I wanted to continue my career in England. I was as shocked as anyone.

"It wasn't an easy decision to make. I'd returned to Sweden for family reasons. I had young children and I wanted them to be brought up close to their family.

"It wasn't something I could decide on my own and we had a family meeting to discuss it. If they hadn't wanted me to carry on, I would have put my boots away quite happily.

"In the end, though, everyone was happy for me to return to England for a couple of seasons."

Nilsson left Yorkshire intending to combine playing part-time football with a career in the Swedish fire service. It did not quite work out that way.

"Selling insurance was a more convenient option and it was enjoyable," says Roland. "I plan to go back into it when I eventually decide to call it a day.

"I was selling mainly to sports people, from footballers to ice hockey players. It was nice to lead a more normal life.

"I was still enjoying my football and although I wasn't really testing myself week-in-week-out, my standards weren't slipping too much. I felt I was playing as well as ever.

"The training in Sweden was hard and I was just as fit as I'd been in England. I trained before and after work. I knew I could still do myself justice in the Premiership.

"Although I didn't miss the lifestyle, I did begin to miss the football in England. There isn't the same depth of quality back home.

"English football is on the television a lot in Sweden and, every time I watched it, part of me was sad that I was no longer a part of it. I began to think 'what if?'

"Then Coventry stepped in. They gave me a wonderful opportunity and I was determined to make the most of it."

Last season saw the perennial strugglers sail in previously uncharted waters. In the top half of the Premiership table for long stretches of the campaign, thoughts switched from survival to European football qualification. It also led Nilsson to reconsider his future.

He goes on, "I'm enjoying my football more than ever. I've treated this as a bonus to my career and it has been even better than I imagined.

"When I arrived at Highfield Road my intention was to see out my two-year contract and then retire from football for good. I'm having second thoughts now.

"Things have gone well personally and for the team and I might want to carry on a little bit longer. Any decision, though, will be up to the club. They might not want to keep me.

"If Gordon Strachan wants me to stay, I would definitely consider it very carefully. We will just have to wait and see what happens.

"I can see exciting times ahead for Coventry and I'd love to be a part of any success. I won the League Cup at Sheffield Wednesday and would like nothing more than to mark my retirement with another medal.

"I didn't know what to expect when I first joined. The club was used to relegation battles. I wondered if I might be in for a struggle.

"Then the team got on a roll and thoughts of relegation suddenly lifted. People began to look at the club in a different light.

"The only thing that could hold us back is a negative frame of mind. Coventry have struggled against the drop for years and it is difficult for the club and players to change their outlook.

"I noticed that instead of looking at the possibilities that could stem from a good run of results, people tended to look at the teams below us to see how many points we needed to stay up.

"When we achieved safety, results dropped off because we relaxed. That has to change if the club is to win things. The club has shown that it can beat the best. Now it has to press on and do it more consistently." ■

> ## "I thought I was walking out on English football for good."

going...going...
gong!

Imagine if you had in your possession the first-ever England strip, countless FA Cup and Scottish Cup winners' medals, caps, photographs and other memorabilia worth thousands of pounds.

Well, if you are Grant MacDougall of CHRISTIE'S AUCTIONEERS the dream becomes a distinct reality. Grant is in charge of Christie's annual auction of football memorabilia and over the years has seen the coveted

"The most valuable item was the Sheriff of London Charity Shield, 1897-1907. This was the forerunner to the present day Charity Shield and was competed for by the best amateur and professional sides of the season.

"Once it disappeared north of the border when the famous Scottish amateur side Queen's Park won the right to represent the Amateurs in the 1889 Final v Aston Villa. After a goalless draw the trophy was shared by the two sides.

"It fetched £26,000 in auction."

collections of some of soccer's legends pass through his hands - legends like Alex James, Bill Foulkes, Dixie Dean and Danny Blanchflower.

"I'm a great Rangers fan and I was thrilled when the former Ibrox captain, Eric Caldow, put his collection up for auction," says Grant.

Since the first auction in 1989, the event has gained in popularity every year, culminating in 1998's sale which raised over £301,000, compared to £50,000 in the opening year.

"Not all medals and collections are auctioned simply to raise cash for the owner," says Grant.

"Quite often, the owner prefers his medals to be housed in a collection rather than gather dust in a bank vault or run the risk of burglary

at home. You can't insure these things for sentimental value."

Ray Kennedy, the ex-Arsenal and Liverpool star who developed Parkinson's disease, auctioned his medal collection and the £80,000 raised went into a trust fund for his children.

Grant has seen many unusual items go through the auction process as well as regular memorabilia.

"The funniest was a Blackburn Rovers season ticket from the 1890s which had been won in a competition. The winner was given free life entry to Rovers' home matches, but it was won by a non-football fan. The problem was that it was non-transferrable and therefore never used!"

Although Grant is in charge of the football memorabilia sales, his main job is in the furniture department.

"You could say that the football side of things is a labour of love, because I spend much of my spare time researching items put up for sale. Sometimes, it's the story BEHIND the medal that makes it especially valuable.

"The sad thing is that no one knows just how much history has been lost in medals melted down for gold.

"Of all the 50 FA Cup medals to pass through Christie's sales, only five or so have been 19th Century.

"Of course, some medals are far easier to come across. Celtic and Rangers cup medals are comparatively common but there is a great scarcity of non Old Firm medals."

One of the more outstanding items in last year's auction was one of the first England strips, worn by Arnold Kirke-Smith in the first Scotland-England match, in Glasgow, on the 30th of November, 1872. Valued at £3,500, it went to a private buyer for £18,500!

Is there any item Grant would like to see sold at a Christie's auction?

"That's an easy one," says Grant, "A 1966 World Cup Winner's medal!" Maybe one day... ■

England strip, 1872

Eric Caldow's medals

mixed emotions

feeling good...

feeling good...

● Last season was a roller-coaster ride of emotions for Arsenal's Ian Wright. Beating Cliff Bastin's 52-year-old Arsenal goal-scoring record and winning the League and FA Cup Double with the Gunners were tempered by a series of injuries which caused him to miss a considerable part of the season and most important of all, a trip to France with England for the World Cup.

These pictures sum up the highs and lows of Ian's season.

Injury in a friendly against Morocco — and Ian is out of Glenn Hoddle's World Cup plans.

feeling bad...

● EVERY YEAR THEY BURST ON TO THE FOOTBALL SCENE ... THE TALENTED YOUNGSTERS WHO GO ON TO BECOME SOCCER SUPERSTARS. JUST THINK OF SOME OF THE NAMES WHO HAVE MADE THE SOCCER HEADLINES IN RECENT SEASONS...LIKE DAVID BECKHAM, MICHAEL OWEN AND RIO FERDINAND. BUT WHO WILL BE THE NEXT TO MAKE IT TO THE TOP? TO FIND OUT, WE ASKED FIVE MEN WITH INSIDE KNOWLEDGE OF THE GAME — THEN ADDED A FEW NAMES OF OUR OWN.

tips for the top

FRANK McLINTOCK (ex-Arsenal) Joe Cole (West Ham United)

"I first saw Joe as a fifteen-year-old trialist, and he looked better than some first-team players!

"He has everything...energy, pace, skill... the lot. I rate him to be the best schoolboy I have seen.

"Liverpool's Michael Owen is another who has it all. He reminds me a bit of the great Denis Law. It's good to see someone with a bit of fire in his belly."

BARRY DAVIES (BBC Commentator) Harry Kewell (Leeds United)

"Harry seems to have huge amounts of natural talent as well as considerable verve and enthusiasm.

"There's not too much he can't do and he's a huge prospect for Leeds. The only regret is that he's Australian and not available for one of the home nations."

BOBBY GOULD (Wales coach)

"Two Welsh youngsters who I believe have bright futures are Matty Jones of Leeds United and Daniel Gabbidon of West Bromwich Albion.

"Matty is a strong competitor and a good footballer who plays anchorman in the midfield. He has a lot of passion and he will be a very good international player.

"There are good club players and good international players. Sometimes the two don't mix, but Matty is a good enough player to be able to feel comfortable at club and international level.

"Gabbidon is a super defender. He has tremendous pace, more pace than I have seen in any of the Welsh defenders I have worked with for the last two-and-a-half years.

"I have no shadow of a doubt about these two lads. When Daniel breaks into the first-team at West Brom, people will say 'Where has he come from?'. I'm just delighted that we have him in the Welsh set-up.

"Craig Bellamy (left) and Chris Llewellyn of Norwich have

Continued over page

also broken through. They have both been outstanding for their club.

"You look at a lad like Michael Owen, who has been superb, but Craig, who scored on his Wales debut in Malta in June, and Chris are not far off that level. They are both talented young lads who can also make a very big impression with both club and country."

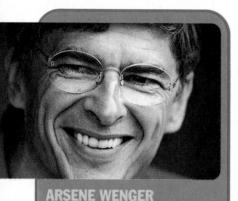

ARSENE WENGER
(Arsenal manager)
Nicolas Anelka (Arsenal)

"I believe that Nicolas will very soon become a world class attacker. He had a difficult time when he first arrived at Arsenal, but is learning all the time. Nicolas has improved his fighting spirit, and now realises how hard he has to work at this level. He resists tackles much better, and is attuned to the style of the team.

"Of course, inexperienced players sometimes make mistakes. But that is how they learn. Nicolas is very young. He is a talent who can only improve with experience. One or two of the goals he scored for us last season were top class. His finishing is very cool, but of course his biggest asset is his pace which makes it very hard for defenders to catch him."

ALEX FERGUSON
(Manchester United manager)
Wes Brown (Manchester United)

United manager Alex Ferguson is expecting big things from the latest youngster to break through at Old Trafford. Wes Brown, a teenager who can play at either full-back or centre-half, made his League debut against Leeds United last May.

"We have great hopes for Wes," says Ferguson. "I brought him off the bench to make his debut, but I would have had no qualms about playing him from the start. The lad would have handled it no problem.

"He is at a good club to come through because fans at Old Trafford really appreciate

youngsters. They have been brought up on young lads coming through the ranks and they will take to lads like Wes.

"He has the raw attributes, but he needs to put a bit of meat on the bones. That will come with age, though."

Here are another five young men to keep an eye on...

GAVIN McCANN (EVERTON)

McCann was overshadowed by the likes of Danny Cadamarteri, Michael Ball and John Oster at Goodison Park last season, but as the campaign neared its end, McCann had become a regular in the starting eleven.

The midfielder had to learn his trade the hard way as Everton fought against relegation, but that experience will make him a stronger player in future.

NEIL ROBERTS (WREXHAM)

Has yet to make it onto the Premiership scene, but few doubt that the Wrexham striker will grace the top flight in the near future.

Wrexham manager Brian Flynn carefully nurtured the local lad last term with regular substitute appearances, but an injury crisis forced him to give Roberts his full debut and the then 19-year-old scored twice. He also scored in each of the next three games to further enhance his reputation. Flynn continued to pick and choose the youngster's appearances, but Roberts will soon make himself a first-team regular.

HASNEY ALJOFREE (BOLTON)

Aljofree made his Bolton Wanderers debut against Blackburn towards the end of last season and immediately looked like a star of the future.

The Manchester-born left-back is quick enough to match the best wingers, but his main asset is his tenacity in the tackle. Although not as powerful as somebody like Stuart Pearce, Aljofree is not afraid to make his presence felt.

KENNY LUNT (CREWE)

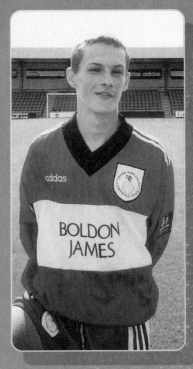

England's Under-18 skipper could be following in the footsteps of Danny Murphy, who moved from Crewe to Liverpool last season.

Like Murphy, Lunt is an attacking midfielder, highly rated by Gresty Road boss Dario Gradi, whose track record in producing young talent is second to none.

FA Technical Director Howard Wilkinson, who is also in charge of the England Under-18 side, echoes Gradi's view.

MATT HOLLAND (IPSWICH)

Discarded by West Ham as a youngster, Matt drifted into non-League football before being picked up by Bournemouth. A midfielder with an eye for goal and a tremendous shot, he joined George Burley's young squad in the summer of 1997.

oyvind leonhardsen
liverpool

phil neville
manchester united

it's a funny old game

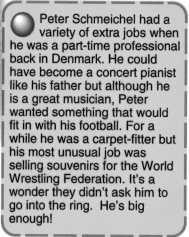

Peter Schmeichel had a variety of extra jobs when he was a part-time professional back in Denmark. He could have become a concert pianist like his father but although he is a great musician, Peter wanted something that would fit in with his football. For a while he was a carpet-fitter but his most unusual job was selling souvenirs for the World Wrestling Federation. It's a wonder they didn't ask him to go into the ring. He's big enough!

Premiership new boys Charlton Athletic have come a long way since they played at Woolwich Common earlier this century. In those days they had to change in dressing rooms which were a mile from the pitch - and they had to carry the goal-posts the same distance both before and after the game!

If you find yourself watching football on television in Argentina, watch out if a penalty is awarded. The television shows a cartoon referee walking across the screen ... led by a guide dog!

If at first you don't succeed try, try, and try again. That could certainly be said for Iran's quest for France 98. When they beat Australia for the final qualification place, it was their third attempt at qualification. Failure at the group stage was followed by defeat by Japan before they eliminated Terry Venables' Socceroos. All the effort was worth it, though, when they won one of their First Round matches, beating the United States 2-1.

"I JUST ASKED HIM IF HE COULD DO ANY BETTER!"

"THAT MIGHT BE YOUR OPINION BUT I THINK I HAD A GREAT GAME!"

"MAYBE MR HODDLE WILL GIVE ME A GAME IN GOAL!"

"...ON THE OTHER HAND MAYBE NOT!"

"ZZZZZ!"

"IT'S THE ONLY WAY I CAN PUT A SWERVE ON THE BALL!"

In 1875, a whaling crew decided to enjoy their Christmas Day by playing football on an ice-floe. The game was in full swing when an extra player turned up - a full-grown male polar bear! He began chasing the ball but found that he was suddenly having to play on his own, the whalers having run back to their ship!

Some strange games were played during the war years. In the Wartime Cup, Stockport played Doncaster on March 23rd, 1946, and it was decided by the organisers that there would have to be a result on the day, no matter how long it took. The game was abandoned, though, with the score at 2-2. The two teams had played for eight hours and twenty minutes, and they just could not go on any longer!

"HEY, REF HE'S WEARING MY STRIP!"

"HEY! CAN I HAVE MY LEG BACK PLEASE?"

There were tacos flying when Tampico-Marero took on Puebla in a Mexican League match recently. A taco seller disagreed with a linesman's offside decision and began pelting him with his wares. He ran out of tacos before officials jumped on him. The linesman was unconcerned but later said he would have preferred to have had the tacos thrown at him AFTER the game.

NIALL QUINN'S Sunderland

wear and

IALL QUINN and Kevin Phillips were the toast of the new Stadium of Light last season.

The Sunderland forwards struck fear into the hearts of First Division defences, helping the club end up as top scorers in the Division.

Phillips created a real splash in his first season at the club following his bargain £625,000 move from Watford. He grabbed most of the attention as he set a new club record of scoring in seven successive games on the way to being the Wearsiders' top scorer. He finished up with 36 goals, breaking Brian Clough's post-war aggregate record in the process.

Quinn's contribution was equally significant, if not quite so loudly trumpeted. Most of Phillips' goals came courtesy of a Quinn assist.

The roaring approval of a packed 40,000 home crowd sounded particularly sweet for the big Irishman. Just a year earlier, he was derided as the club slid from the top division. More seriously, he faced the very real threat of having his career ended by a serious knee injury.

Says the Republic of Ireland international, "I had a nightmare start to my Sunderland career. Within eight games of signing me for £1 million - a lot of money for the club at the time - I suffered a serious cruciate ligament injury.

"It was the second such injury I'd had in my career having suffered the same problem at Manchester City. I was devastated. Moving to Sunderland was supposed to represent a new start for me. I was desperate to do well. I was just beginning to get among the goals as the club started the Premiership season pretty well. Then the injury came.

"I had an operation and was doing the usual rehabilitation as the club plummeted towards the relegation zone. I felt really guilty. Peter Reid had bought me to score the goals to help the club stay in the division but I was proving to be a disastrous buy.

"Naturally, the fans weren't too happy with the way things were going and were looking for people to blame. I got my share of stick. I was so desperate to prove myself to these people that I flogged myself to get fit. I must have set some kind of world record by getting back in five months.

"I pushed myself so I could help the club in the final run-in to the Premiership season. The gaffer

> ## "My knee was in a terrible state and for six weeks I didn't know if I'd play ever again."

hadn't had much luck in the transfer market and I saw he needed a hand.

"I wasn't really ready and people close to me told me I wouldn't get any thanks for coming back too soon. The people who had used radio phone-ins to say that I was always injured and at Sunderland just for the money annoyed me. I was desperate to give it a go.

"Initially the team's results improved but it proved to be too little too late and we went down on the final day of the season. I was inconsolable. My gamble hadn't paid off because I re-injured the knee during the summer. In fact my career was nearly ended because I was so eager to help Sunderland.

"When the fans heard about my situation, some had another go and questioned my

commitment to the club. That really hurt me. That was the least of my troubles, though. My knee was in a terrible state and for six weeks I didn't know if I'd play ever again.

"The surgeon who opened the knee found that the fibula and tibia had fused and there was no flexibility in my knee. He chipped bone from both sides and told me that it might work, or it might fuse again in a few weeks. If it didn't work, he made it clear he wouldn't operate again. I'd had seven major operations on it in seven years and another would cause me major problems later in life.

"That period where I didn't know one way or another if it would work was the worst of my life. I couldn't just hide in a corner and think that my career wouldn't be over. I had to face the fact that I might not play ever again. At one stage I couldn't see any improvement at all and I was very pessimistic. Bit by bit, though, it improved and my confidence grew.

"I had a spur to prove my doubters wrong. I couldn't have been more motivated in my recovery.

"I had a great rapport with the fans at Manchester City and wanted to have something similar with the Sunderland fans. I knew that as long as I was fully fit, I could achieve that.

"This time the operation was a complete success. For the first time in years I could kick the ball properly instead of just side-footing everything. I also found an unusual benefit of my previous inactivity. I must have been the only player to come back from injury and lose weight!

"I returned to the team three-quarters of a stone lighter than when I last played. The reason was that I had stopped the weight training I'd started at City to improve my strength.

"When I returned to action last November, I was in peak health and fitness.

"Playing with Kevin was perfect. I'm at my best when I'm playing with someone who sniffs out my flicks and knock-ons. We are a great team.

"I didn't know much about Kevin when he arrived but he learned a lot last season and gets better with every game.

"He is our main goalscorer and I'm happy to help him along." ∎

days could have ended in disaster!

tears!

fantas

Pinch me, I'm dreaming! says Barnsley's

WHEN unfashionable Barnsley won promotion to the Premiership two seasons ago, that unaccustomed success sparked one of the biggest celebrations in English football

It also kicked off a magic carpet ride for the devotees of the South Yorkshire club, who spent the whole of last season revelling in the joys of entertaining giants such as Manchester United, Arsenal and Liverpool, and visiting the country's top venues.

Manager Danny Wilson's side may have been at the bottom of the table for most of the campaign, but that did not dampen the spirit of the fans who were determined to enjoy their time among the elite, come what may.

But if the fans were in Dreamland, it was sheer fantasy for midfield grafter Darren Sheridan, who spent his campaign in the top flight wondering if it was all really happening.

Darren was a late-comer to the professional game, having been picked up from non-League football at the age of 26, learning his trade scrapping against the cloggers in a Sunday pub league.

Ironically, Sheridan cites this experience as the one which turned him into a real footballer and made him the player he is today.

But while he was undergoing that process, he was living a life as far removed as you could imagine from the glamour of being a Premiership player.

While many of the stars

football

DARREN SHERIDAN

who shared a pitch with him last season were already clocking up their first century of League appearances, Darren was moving from one dead-end job to another, uncertain of where his next pay packet was coming from.

Having been rejected by Leeds United as a teenager, he drifted into whatever short-term employment he could find. He laid tarmac, humped sackfuls of mail through the Manchester rain and sweated it out on a building site.

No wonder, when he looks back on his route to the top, he still finds it hard

> "To play at places like Old Trafford and White Hart Lane has been like a dream come true for me."

to believe his current status.

Says Darren, "To play at places like Old Trafford and White Hart Lane and face the best players in the Premiership every week has been like a dream come true for me.

"A decade ago, after Leeds had let me go, I would never have thought this could happen.

"I had spent two years at Elland Road after leaving school and when their manager at the time, the late Billy Bremner, told me that I didn't figure in his plans and was being released, I said simply, 'Fair

enough.'

"But I went home that day with a broken heart and all my dreams shattered, feeling that my world had ended. I thought, 'I'm not good enough, so nobody else will want me.'

"I just started messing around with my mates and drifted into one part-time job after another. I did a stint of laying tarmac, and when that finished I did all sorts of other jobs. For a while I was a labourer, then a postman. I even spent a few months working as a baker.

"It was all short-term contract work and rarely full-time. Every six months, I seemed to find myself at the end of a contract, looking for something new.

"It was a million miles away from the life I had aimed to achieve while I was at Elland Road, yet that kept coming back to haunt me.

"Every time I switched on the television to watch Match of the Day, it seemed to feature a player with whom I had done my apprenticeship.

"David Batty had been a year behind me, yet there he was, doing extremely well. So was Gary Speed, who had been there at the same time.

"My one consolation was that my brother, John, was among them, starring for Leeds and winning caps for the Republic of Ireland.

"John arrived at Elland Road for a trial while I was an apprentice there, and they signed him up straight away.

"Though I was so upset that I didn't make it, I knew that was purely down to me. But I was delighted for John that he made the grade. I used to watch him a lot and was so pleased for him."

Meanwhile, Darren

slipped into the world of Sunday pub football and now believes it was the making of him. But it took the sharp eye of a manager from the Unibond League to recognise the potential and knock him into shape.

"Playing Sunday football helped turn me into the player I am now," admits Darren. "I am now much more of a battler, ironically trying to play in a similar style to the man who became something of a role model for me.

"Though Billy Bremner was the man who rejected me at Leeds, I had a lot of admiration for him. In those days, he still joined in all the practice matches in training and whenever I watched him play it was obvious what a great player he had been, and he still had a bit of football in him.

"In those days, however, I was the complete opposite. I saw myself as a ball player, and certainly wasn't a tackler.

"In fact, I probably wasn't serious enough about my football and didn't put nearly enough into my game. That was probably a major reason for Billy letting me go.

"However, playing Sunday football against pub teams sorted me out. There were a lot of hard, physical lads in that league, who thought nothing of clattering you at every opportunity. I was battered about, spent a lot of time on the deck and ended up with plenty of bruises.

"But you soon get used to that and, after three years of playing in that company, I was giving as good as I was getting."

The transformation was spotted by Mike McKenzie, then manager of Unibond League side, Winsford

United, who took Darren under his wing.

"I owe a lot to Mike, who is now boss of Hyde United in the same league," says Sheridan. "He had been the manager of another Sunday League side whom I had played against and when he moved to Saturday football with Winsford, he asked me to join them.

"He had seen the physical streak which had developed in me, and believed that he could help me make it. He was absolutely brilliant with me and gave me the kick up the backside which I needed and pushed me along.

"I couldn't drive in those days, but he picked me up in the evenings and took me to training. Then he drove me through each session, forced me to do the hard work and got me fit.

"That higher level of fitness, allied to the hard streak I'd picked up in pub football, must have helped me get noticed by Barnsley.

"Now, even after almost six years at Oakwell, I still regard it as unbelievable that I made it into top-level football.

"I have viewed it as a second bite at the cherry and treat every match in that way.

"When Barnsley took me on, I decided that I had better take my chance this time, so I got my head down and worked hard. I am much more conscientious than I was at Leeds. But I have also resolved to enjoy the opportunity and make the most of it.

"I have mates who come to watch me who have just come off 10-hour shifts. I have been there and I know which is the best life, so I am determined to hang on to it for as long as I can." ∎

scot gemmill
nottingham forest

ONE way or another, Steve Harper is determined to enjoy a career in football. The goalkeeper, who spent most of last season out on loan at First Division Huddersfield Town from Newcastle Utd, looks to have a bright future ahead of him.

Unable to break into the first team at St James Park, Harper received plenty of plaudits for his performances at the McAlpine Stadium.

If he does not make it, however, Harper has no intention of walking away from the game. He will merely change out of his goalkeeping kit and step

who'd be a ref?
I would, says STEVE HARPER

into his referee's uniform.

Having passed his Class Three exam in the summer of 1997, Harper is, as far as anyone knows, the only player currently on the books of a Premiership club who is also a referee.

Although it is just a pastime at the moment, he sees it as a useful string to his bow.

Says Steve, "I used to run a Sunday morning pub team, the Half Moon in Easington, in the Peterlee and District League. There were so many occasions when the referee didn't turn up.

"I used to step in, with the agreement of both sides, and officiate. I enjoyed it and everyone said I was better than the usual refs. That set me thinking.

"My Uncle Barry had been a referee for 27 years in the local area and was unfortunate not to make it on to the the

> **"In one game, I gave a penalty against my next-door neighbour."**

League lists.

"I watched a few games where he officiated and the respect he commanded from the players was great. He was well thought of and that influenced me to give it a go.

"At the end of season 1996-'97, I passed my exams. I thought it might be a good thing, even if I only earned a certificate from it but I've now caught the bug.

"It's a hobby but I take it seriously. There is talk of professional referees and, if my playing career comes to nothing, you never know what the future might hold.

"People say that I must be crazy but it suits me. With me, abuse goes in one ear and out of the other."

Steve's refereeing career began in the Peterlee and District League and after his early experiences the pressure of officiating in a Wembley cup final would pale into insignificance.

Steve goes on, "I'm not scared to put yellow cards in the faces of my friends. I've already upset a few of them with some of my decisions.

"I've refereed the team I used to run a few times and, in one game, I gave a penalty against my next-door neighbour, who took over running the side from me. They

ended up drawing the game.

"There were a few lads giving me a bit of stick but it was definitely a penalty. The referee is never wrong!

"I used to have a reputation as a ref who didn't book people. Then I took charge of an Under-15 game and a couple of lads started having a pushing match. I split them up and thought that would be the end of it.

> ## "One of the kids also used to be a next-door neighbour of mine. I remember him being born and there I was sending him off!"

"Unfortunately they tried to strangle each other and one of them was trying to head-butt the other. Both of them had to be sent off.

"One of the kids also used to be a next-door neighbour of mine. I remember him being born and there I was sending him off!

"Under-15 games are probably the hardest to take because they think they know it all and are the hardest people in the world."

Harper is adamant that his secondary role has been helpful to his playing career.

He explains, "You'd be surprised what

professional footballers don't know about the laws of the game.

"I quite often put certain situations to fellow players and ask them what they'd do if they were refereeing.

The number of times they've been wrong is unbelievable.

"It's worth doing just from the point of view of not being caught out by the laws."

Harper also defends his fellow officials in the wake of the debate about a lowering in refereeing standards.

"I think the referees in the First Division are of a good quality," says Steve. "Unless you've actually been out there and done it yourself, you can't begin to understand the level of abuse refs take. It's unfair because we're only human beings.

"I always make a point of passing on my best wishes to the assistant referees when they check the nets before a game and I make sure I shake the ref's hand after a game. Only those who've done it know how hard it is." ◼

habit forming!

Fr. John Seddon

aLLSPORT, one of the UK's leading photographic agencies, has joined forces with Keyhaven International, a management company specialising in indexing, cataloguing and data entry, to caption thousands of photographic images every week. Not just football, but dozens of sports from shinty to show-jumping!

Keyhaven use the expertise of an unlikely band of men for this specialist and accurate work. Not sports writers or computer whizz-kids — but monks!

From the 11th century, monks have been largely self-sufficient and have supported themselves through education, agriculture and, more traditionally, by the illumination of manuscripts and documentation copying. As we move towards the 21st century they have developed these skills further to include computer-orientated tasks. The nature of the captioning work requires patience, accuracy and thoroughness which, historically,

Simon Moran and Les Symes (Allsport), Natasha Volkers (Keyhaven), and some of the St Augustine's "Team".

■ *Fr. Dunstan Keauffling*

■ *Fr. John Seddon Simon Moran,*
Fr. Dunstan Keauffling

are synonymous with monastic life.

The use of monks to undertake this work was pioneered in the UK by the monks of St. Augustine's Abbey, in Ramsgate.

The monks receive the cropped and colour corrected images on a disk containing up to 1,000 pictures, supported by copies of the original transparency and corresponding barcode. Within the monastery the monks have computers capable of running Allsport's custom- written software from which they can view the images and individually caption them. They rely on reference books, the original caption and their own expert knowledge to build up the Allsport caption.

Father Dunstan Keauffling is the bursar at St. Augustine's, where he spends much of his working day looking after the finances and the general day-to-day running of the monastery.

He is a sports enthusiast, and

has interesting memories of being taught how to play football by Trevor Brooking.

"Sadly his coaching skills were not as adept as his playing skills and my footballing career was short-lived!" says Father Dunstan.

Monks in the United States have been working with Allsport USA on captioning their images for the past 18 months. The Allsport Archive is a combination of both Allsport UK and Allsport USA's images. ■

collectors corner

eVERY June, the International Football Memorabilia and Programme Fair is held at the Russell Hotel in London's Russell Square. The 1999 event will be its 25th anniversary, which makes it a mere baby when compared to the age of most of the items at the Fair.

Every Football League team is represented in some way, and many non-League ones as well, plus England, Scotland, Wales and Northern Ireland international programmes.

On show at the 1998 Fair was a Southampton programme from 1904 owned by Roy Calmels (below). This was priced at £400 but was by no means the most expensive there. That belonged to Richard Cohen who had an Arsenal v Cardiff City Cup Final programme from 1927 worth £700. And they say the present-day Cup Final programmes are expensive!

But there are some bargains to be found and even if you don't bring your wallet, you're bound to find something of interest to browse through.

The Fair is organised by The Football Programme Directory who will deal with any enquiries you may have about a programme you need for your collection. You can join their organisation for £11 and receive a monthly magazine which will give you information on any forthcoming programmes fairs in your area.

● Richard Cohen with two of his most expensive programmes. Austria v England, from 1936 (worth £650) and the Arsenal v Cardiff Cup Final programme.

Write to *David Stacey, The Football Programme Directory, 66 Southend Road, Wickford, Essex, SS11 8EN.*

●*Young with old. 12-year-old Gary Thake (West Ham, left) and Kevin Thomson, 10, (Arsenal) hold up programmes of their favourites from modern day to yesteryear. Gary has a Hammers programme from 1964 and Kevin's is a Highbury match played in 1936.*

david hopkin
leeds united

Why Keith Blackwell doesn't mind getting the bird!

HERE are two sides to Crystal Palace supporter Keith Blackwell. Monday to Friday, he is the sober-suited, responsible headmaster of Churchill Primary School, in Kent.

But come Saturday, he runs around Selhurst Park in fancy-dress costume, kitted out as a giant soccer-playing eagle!

Keith is one of football's anonymous heroes. The brave souls who parade around football grounds before kick-off, hidden inside cumbersome clobber, stirring up support and entertaining fans.

A Palace fan from the age of nine, Keith answered an advertisement in the Palace programme three years ago for somebody prepared to take on the arduous role of wearing the heavy Eagle outfit at Selhurst Park.

"The previous incumbent was having heart problems. I went for an interview, and was offered the

> "My son, Tom, now 21, wasn't too impressed at the time. He was a bit embarrassed at his dad parading around Crystal Palace in an Eagle outfit."

job," reveals Keith.

"I didn't tell my wife Vanessa until afterwards. But she's very tolerant, and accepts it as part of life.

"My son, Tom, now 21, wasn't too impressed at the time. He was a bit embarrassed at his dad parading around Crystal Palace in an Eagle outfit.

"But when Coca-Cola approached us to do a television advert it was a bit different. Tom was filmed peeling Brussels sprouts, while talking about the double life of his father the headmaster and the Palace mascot.

"Now he can laugh about it, and he's quite proud of me. I think the same goes for the pupils at my school.

"It's rather nice that they respect the difference between me at school and at the football club. They know where to draw the line, but it was quite amusing how they found out.

"Soon after I took over the role, Crystal Palace players came to the school as part of the Football in the Community scheme. It was a six-week course of talking to the children, doing some coaching, and that kind of thing.

"At the end, they gave the school 100 match tickets for a game against Wolves. As I was doing my stuff before the game, I realised one or two of the kids recognised me, because up close you can see my face through the Eagle's beak.

"I could hear them saying, 'It is him, I know it's him.' At school on the Monday morning, they said 'Hello, Sir, we saw you at Crystal Palace.'

"The children accept that I can be headmaster at school, but at Selhurst Park I can have a joke with them and there is a dividing line.

"I see my role as being there to entertain. To keep the kids happy and make people chuckle.

"Some mascots just walk around and wave. I like to go up and talk to the fans. I will go to the away fans, but I have to sum up the mood first. I'm not there to antagonise.

"I saw the role described as 'the saddest job alive' in a newspaper. I had to write in.

"I think the mascot projects the image of the club. There is a fine line between amusement and ridicule, and you have to be careful to stay on the right side.

"I didn't feel foolish the first time I did it. I was just very nervous. I didn't want to make a fool of myself.

"But it's every fan's ambition to get on the pitch with the players. I enjoy the contact. The players are amused, and some always have a few words.

"I've been to Wembley twice, for the Play-off Finals, but I don't go to many away grounds. I don't like encroaching on somebody else's territory, although I'm happy to welcome other mascots to

Making friends with the Leicester Fox!

Selhurst Park.

"We have to get changed in a small room under the stand. When we played Leicester City, the Fox came to Selhurst Park. Their mascot is a woman, but there was no problem about getting changed in the same room. My wife was there to help us both!

"The Eagle outfit is very heavy, and I often get very hot. I sweat off pounds each game. When the costume wears out, we will look at getting a fibre-glass frame which will be lighter to wear."

But for the time being, Keith Blackwell is happy to carry the burden of the Eagle outfit, while lightening the atmosphere at Selhurst Park.

Proving that football can be fun and headmasters can be game for a laugh. ∎

a tale of two cities

a t the end of last season, Shaun Goater must have felt like the man who withdrew from the Lottery syndicate just before it hit the jackpot!

The Manchester City striker's decision to leave Bristol City for Maine Road on transfer deadline day last March looked like a gamble at the time, but the full extent of Goater's decision did not hit home until his new club were relegated to the Second Division on the final day of the season.

While the Maine Road men dropped a division, Goater's former team-mates in Bristol won promotion and traded places with Joe Royle's side.

Despite beating Stoke 5-2 in their last game of the campaign, City could not prevent relegation to the third tier of English football for the first time in their 111-year history.

To make matters worse for Goater, a last-day defeat for Bristol City meant he lost out on two fronts.

Says the Bermudan striker, "When I signed for Manchester City, I knew the club was in a bad position in the League, but I didn't see the move as a gamble. I still don't.

"No club is too good or too big to go down and we found that out for ourselves. I fully expected City to stay up, but despite the risks, I came to Maine Road because it was a great career opportunity.

"When you play in front of 32,000 people every other week, it is very hard to get any bigger than that. I didn't expect to be back in the Second Division so quickly, but even though we went down, this club is bigger than Bristol City and that's why I came here.

"We had six games to save ourselves when I arrived and I thought we would do it. I actually believed we would stay up quite easily. Unfortunately, I was proved wrong.

"Even before we went down, people were telling me that I had made a mistake by coming to City. I had left Bristol City when they were virtually guaranteed promotion to the First Division.

"If I had stayed at Ashton Gate, I would have been playing First Division football this season. I put that on the line when I came to Manchester and ended up back in the Second Division.

"I even missed out on a Second Division Championship medal with Bristol City. They were looking good for the title, but they slipped up in the final week and lost out to Watford. If they had won the division, I would have received a medal.

"I know I made the right move, however. About nine years ago, I came over from Bermuda to play for Manchester United after Old Trafford manager Alex Ferguson spotted me in a tour game.

"From my time across the city, I know just how big the two Manchester clubs are. Coming to City was a good move and, hopefully, time will prove me right.

"Despite my time at Old Trafford, I don't really consider myself as a former United player. Although I was on the books there, I never progressed further than the reserve team.

"When people ask me, I tell them that my first club was Rotherham United. After two years at Old Trafford, I moved to Rotherham and that's where I feel as though I served my apprenticeship.

"I had a great time at Old Trafford and made some good friends in Lee Sharpe and Mark Robins. However, I didn't learn about the English game and the tactics involved until I went to Rotherham.

"They helped me become the player I am today and I really want to prove myself at a higher level after playing virtually all of my football in the bottom two divisions. This time next year, I want to say I am a First Division player again." ■

122

braveheart!
COLIN HENDRY— the Flying Scotsman

● Colin Hendry displays the all-action style that makes him one of the most respected centre-backs in the world.

steve fulton
hearts

picture list

ISBN 0 85116 6644

Printed and Published in Great Britain by
D.C. Thomson & Co. Ltd., 185 Fleet Street,
London EC4A 2HS. © D.C. Thomson & Co.
Ltd., 1998.

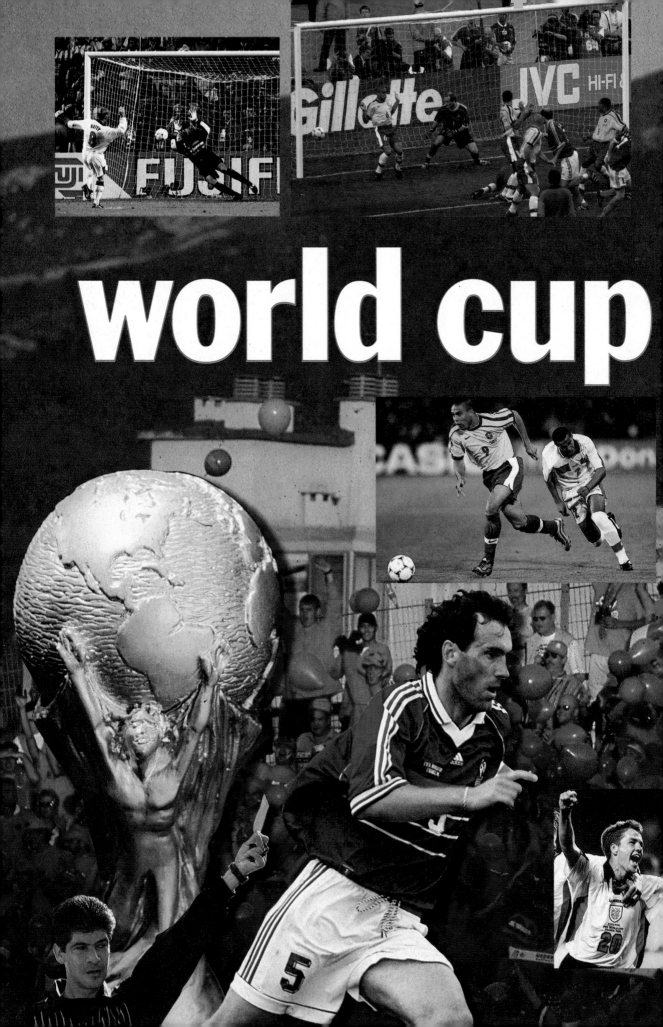

world cup